It's a Yes!

Gráinne Griffin, Orla O'Connor
and Ailbhe Smyth, with
Alison O'Connor

About the Authors

~~~~~~

Gráinne Griffin is one of three female co-directors who led the Together for Yes referendum campaign in Ireland in 2018. Gráinne is a founding member and board member of the Abortion Rights Campaign (ARC), a grassroots, volunteer-led, nationwide organisation, established in 2013 to bring about the introduction of free, safe and legal abortion services to Ireland. In addition to her reproductive rights work, Gráinne has over fifteen years of experience contributing to NGO and activist organisations and currently works as a senior manager developing and funding Irish information and advocacy services. Gráinne was listed as one of *Time*'s 100 Most Influential People in 2019 for her work on the Together for Yes campaign.

Orla O'Connor is Director of the National Women's Council of Ireland (NWCI), the leading national women's membership organisation in Ireland, with over 190 member groups. She was co-director of Together for Yes, the national civil society campaign to remove the Eighth Amendment from the Irish Constitution. For her role in Together for Yes, Orla was recognised as one of *Time*'s 100 Most

Influential People in 2019. Orla is a feminist and an expert in the policies needed to progress women's rights and equality in Ireland. She has led numerous high-level successful campaigns on a wide range of issues on women's rights, including social welfare reform, pension reform and the introduction of quality and affordable childcare. Orla holds an MA in European Social Policy.

Ailbhe Smyth was a co-director of the Together for Yes national referendum campaign. A long-time feminist, LGBTI and socialist activist, she co-founded and is convenor of the Coalition to Repeal the Eighth Amendment and was centrally involved in the marriage equality campaign of 2015. Ailbhe is the former founding head of Women's Studies (the Women's Education, Research and Resource Centre) at University College Dublin, and has published widely on feminism, politics and culture. For her role in Together for Yes, Ailbhe was recognised as one of *Time*'s 100 Most Influential People in 2019.

Alison O'Connor is a journalist, broadcaster, author, mother and feminist. Her work as a political columnist involves regular commentary on current affairs on radio and television. She has a weekly column in the *Irish Examiner*. She previously wrote a book on clerical sex abuse in the Diocese of Ferns, *A Message from Heaven: The Life and Crimes of Father Seán Fortune*.

It's a Yes!

How Together for Yes *Repealed the Eighth and Transformed Irish Society*

Gráinne Griffin, Orla O'Connor
and Ailbhe Smyth, with
Alison O'Connor

ORPEN PRESS

Published by
Orpen Press
Upper Floor, Unit K9
Greenogue Business Park
Rathcoole
Co. Dublin
Ireland

email: info@orpenpress.com
www.orpenpress.com

Paperback ISBN 978-1-78605-080-9
ePub ISBN 978-1-78605-081-6

Printed in Dublin by SPRINTprint Ltd

We dedicate this book to all those who suffered because of the Eighth Amendment.

Acknowledgements

~~~~~~

We would like to thank from the bottom of our hearts the 1.4 million people who voted to repeal the Eighth Amendment, the thousands who campaigned throughout Ireland and the women and couples who courageously shared their stories of the suffering they endured trying to access abortions.

Contents

1

The Leaders

~~~~~~

If there is a common bond between the three women who would eventually lead the toughest and most successful referendum campaign in Ireland it is that they are feminist and their politics decidedly left-wing. Hardly surprising that. While the three come from diverse backgrounds, with a wide age span between them, they were strongly united in their determination to bring about the change which would enable Irish women to access abortion on home soil.

Throughout Ailbhe Smyth's life she has been involved in too many campaigns to remember the details of them all. In a number she was "a foot soldier just out there campaigning and leafleting". Abortion had been a constant in that activist life, but she also fought

1

hard to get the ban lifted on divorce. This was of particular importance since she had to legally remain for many years in a marriage which was long over.

After the loss of the 1986 divorce referendum, where it was proposed to remove the constitutional ban on divorce, she felt utterly devastated, unable to muster her customary pragmatism that even when you lose it's worth the effort of trying. She considered emigrating. "I really thought I can't bear this. I found those years very difficult."

But even recollecting that bleak period she brought to mind a campaigning incident that involved her wearing a sandwich board in the Dublin suburb of Dundrum. It stated: "Please give me a second chance". As she stood there, coming towards her in the distance, she spotted a familiar figure. It was her mother, now deceased, "a devoted Catholic, a deeply conservative woman, but an extraordinary one". Ailbhe laughed as she remembered making a dive for a nearby flowerbed filled with shrubbery. "Nobody should ever say that campaigning isn't funny. During that campaign my mother told me she was voting against divorce, which she did, and again in 1995, even though I said to her, 'Well I need a divorce.'" That second referendum did eventually result in the introduction of divorce in Ireland.

Thinking back, Ailbhe says she was late getting involved in the women's movement because she had been so ill during the first half of the 1970s and spent a lot of time in hospital. "I had very severe anorexia nervosa and also acute clinical depression from the age of about 21 to 29. They often go together. So my twenties were wiped out."

She had a brief marriage at that time "for a six month period, because I thought you must be part of a couple, and married. Of course with no divorce in Ireland I couldn't get unmarried until 1995." During that time she was doing a lot of reading and thinking:

"I began to realise that I was ill because I was a woman and trying to be perfect and achieve everything, and be married and perform well, and be nice to everybody and it was making me very, very sick. But it also opened my eyes to the ways in which you could think about the world, and the ways you could think about women in the world."

As the penny was beginning to drop she had started lecturing in French in University College Dublin (UCD). In the lecture hall she would look around and see almost 300 girls and young women in front of her and about five young men:

"And I wondered to myself why is this? And why also am I in this particular department? Why am I not doing Engineering? Not that I would have been a good engineer, but why this? I began to look at what was happening with women in academic life."

In 1976 she became pregnant, which further developed her thought process. She went into hospital to deliver her baby reading Adrienne Rich's powerful *Of Woman Born: Motherhood as Experience and Institution*.

"Adrienne Rich was explaining there is yourself as a mother and your feelings and emotions and so forth. And then there is the institution of motherhood which is another game entirely and that completely opened my eyes. When my daughter was conceived it was by a woman searching and looking and thinking about feminism, and when she was born she was born to a feminist, because Adrienne Rich changed my mind."

As Ailbhe's daughter, Lydia, grew older during the 1980s her mother began to be become more politically aware and active on issues like contraception, divorce and "the big unspoken", abortion, which led her to involvement in pro-choice politics. In 1983 Ailbhe included a chapter on abortion in her book *Women's Rights in Ireland: A Practical Guide*, probably the first time information on abortion had been published in Ireland. She was here for the beginning of the highly controversial 1983 abortion referendum campaign. At that time Ireland voted on the Eighth Amendment of the Constitution to insert a subsection recognising the equal right to life of the pregnant woman and the unborn, but she was out of the country on sabbatical for a lot of the campaign. While deeply disappointed at the result she does not recall being that shocked.

On her return to UCD Ailbhe set about establishing a Women's Studies programme; the manner in which she gathered people together then would be a sign of future organising abilities.

"I put up notices in UCD asking people to come to a meeting of a Women's Studies Forum on a particular date. People would ask me what was it about. I would say: 'there are loads of people coming; do try and make it.' As it turned out loads of people did. I took it from there. One year, for instance, on December 8th, the Feast of the Immaculate Conception, we had a seminar on new reproductive technologies which were being much criticised, so we were really pushing the boat out. That continued during the 1980s and we did fantastic work and invited in so many women, artists or politicians, who would tell us they had never been invited to speak at UCD before."

Ailbhe believed there are two cornerstones to women's independence and autonomy: one of those is economic, the other is bodily integrity, within which is a woman's right to be safe and secure and not subjected to violence. The other dimension of that is the right of women to make decisions about their own reproductive lives. These were exciting times but they also coincided with the absolute bleakness of 1980s Ireland and the slow progress of the women's movement, not least through so many women emigrating. Ailbhe formally established Women's Studies in UCD in 1990 where she saw her role as enabling women who were interested in thinking differently about gender to look at feminism and work it out for themselves and to go out and do useful and interesting and political things. "Education is always political. I understood that."

Ailbhe would serve as head of the Women's Studies programme from 1990 to 2006. On a wider scale there is no doubt in her mind that her career as an academic was "bruised to the core" not just by her open acknowledgement of her sexuality, but by being pro-choice:

"It wasn't just about being lesbian; to be pro-choice, without even mentioning the word 'abortion', was to be a pariah in Irish society. Ultimately abortion has been the most difficult for feminism and the women's movement and women in this country. This is the issue to which there has been the most resistance, of all the issues women have raised over the years. This is the one in legislative terms that has proved the most intractable. That is not to say we have sorted everything else but it is really the one that was always hardest to do. But that was always a spur to me – if something was really hard to do."

In time the campaigning spirit re-emerged and Ailbhe would stay connected politically from her base as head of Women's Studies in UCD. She would later become involved with People Before Profit.

She remembered how the 1990 election of Mary Robinson as President totally lifted the mood for women in Ireland – "we took off in great style" – but then there was the X Case in 1992 which she was very involved in. That case, one of the most controversial legal battles in the history of the State, saw the High Court prevent a fourteen-year-old girl, who had been raped by a man known to her and her family, from travelling abroad for an abortion. It brought the country, which was convulsed with the controversy, to international attention and was a source of shame for many that a young girl could have been treated in this way in Ireland.

After an appeal to the Supreme Court, the teenager was permitted to travel for an abortion, as her life was deemed to be at risk through the threat of suicide. In the subsequent X Case referendum, Ailbhe was the main spokesperson for the lead campaign organisation Alliance for Choice. On that occasion people were asked to vote on the right to information about abortion, the right to travel to avail of the option, and a third vote on the so-called substantive issue, which modified the Eighth Amendment to prevent the threat of suicide being accepted as a legitimate reason for abortion. The right to information was passed, as well as travel, but the Government's proposal on the substantive issue was rejected. It was effectively a stalemate; however this issue simply would not go away. Despite that Supreme Court ruling, which allowed for the threat of suicide as grounds for abortion, no Government brought forward legislation on the matter.

Just before the referendum that year Ailbhe published an edited collection of essays, *The Abortion Papers: Ireland*. Abortion campaigning was never easy, she recalled:

> "Campaigning for social issues was always a tough task. I remember a lot of occasions when the door was slammed shut, or simply not opened in the first place. There were quite violent responses to you as a person. That was the way it was. In truth I probably was never a great door-to-door person anyway. I just got over-exhausted and excited by it."

Then there were the intervening years when the issue of Irish women travelling abroad for abortions appeared to lie beneath the surface of Irish society – where it was a constant fact but one rarely spoken about out loud:

> "Everyone knew, but nobody was prepared to recognise it. In the Ireland I grew up in women and girls were severely punished for becoming pregnant outside of marriage and hidden away out of sight, out of mind, the so-called 'fallen women'."

But all the time, throughout the decades, it remained on Ailbhe's mind as a campaign that had to be fought and won.

While Ailbhe was running Women's Studies in UCD Orla O'Connor would attend the university to study, beginning in 1987. A middle child of three girls, Orla grew up in Phibsboro in Dublin. Her father was a barman and her mother worked mainly at home, then as a childminder and later in life in the local credit union. Political aware-ness for Orla was first sparked by the anti-apartheid movement and the Dunnes Stores strikers who had refused, in the mid-1980s, to handle South African goods in protest at the regime there. She became a member of the youth organisation of the Workers' Party while a sixth-year student in Loreto College in North Great George's Street. She got a job as a part-time worker in Irish chain store Roches Stores, and as a teenager would become involved in fighting for the rights of part-time workers.

At that time, Orla remembered, there were few employment rights for part-time workers and pay was low. While in college she continued to work part-time and became a union representative. It was a brilliant learning experience, she recalled. In time, while in college, she would be selected to stand as a local election candidate for the Workers' Party in the Cabra ward, but she pulled back from politics when she got the opportunity to study abroad for a Master's degree. During her years in UCD she got much more interested in feminism and active on women's rights:

> "When I was studying social science it was a really good time for thinking and being active on issues of inequality, class and feminism. At that time I got very involved in campaigning for the introduction of a minimum wage, and for part-time workers to have the same rights as full-time employees."

It wasn't an easy time to find a job, but pretty quickly after graduating Orla, as she described it herself, landed a job working with unemployed people and issues surrounding unemployment, in Finglas:

> "This was the early 1990s and there was high unemployment. There was a network of unemployed centres that the Irish Congress of Trade Unions established throughout the country. I was employed as a centre coordinator. Initially it was for a short period of six weeks and it was a sharp learning curve for me. I was working with long-term unemployed men who were experiencing so many difficulties with little chance of finding work and poor State services to support them and their families. The centres operated through the Social Employment schemes,

which were the precursor to the current Community Employment Schemes.

I wanted to continue to study and after a year or so I was successful in securing a place on the first Erasmus programmes from National University of Ireland, Maynooth. It was a European Social Policy Master's and fully funded, which enabled me to participate. I studied in the University of Tilburg in the Netherlands and University of Bath. It was a super experience. I did my thesis on lone parents and their welfare and childcare supports in different EU countries. At that time in Ireland there was no public support for childcare, and it was an enormous barrier for the lone parents I worked with in Finglas. Living in poverty was a constant feature for the lives of lone parents and the stigma of being a lone parent was very evident in Ireland in comparison to other EU countries. After finishing my Master's I returned to Finglas Centre for the Unemployed. I was there for seven years and loved it. I established a community development approach to the work in the centre, which for me was about putting the experiences of women, men and children at the centre of our work. During that time the area-based partnership companies for disadvantaged areas were established. I was very involved in the establishment of the Finglas/Cabra partnership, became a member of the board for ICTU [the Irish Congress of Trade Unions] and was later an ICTU representative on the board of ADM [Area Development Management], a precursor to State agency Pobal. While in these roles I developed a better understanding of inequality and the challenges and resistance to bringing about change. All of this experience gave me a great foundation for my work in the National Women's Council of Ireland [NWCI]."

During that time Orla had many experiences of women needing abortions and support, but there being nothing there for them:

"I spoke with some women who were in their forties on the Community Employment Scheme, about the experiences in their lives, and abortion did come up either in relation to themselves or a member of their family, and how that left them feeling. From that experience I had a deeper understanding of the impact of stigma and shame on women's lives and the devastation that can cause to women throughout their lives. I also met a lot of women who had very difficult lives from the time they were children living in institutions and women who were forced to give up their children. It brought home to me the horrendous treatment of women in our society and the lifelong impact that was having on generations of women."

Orla affiliated the Fingal Centre for the Unemployed to NWCI, the first centre of its kind to become a member. She also became an active member of NWCI herself, although at the time felt the organisation needed to represent the experiences of working-class women and unemployed women to a greater degree. Changes were happening in NWCI, and under the leadership of Noreen Byrne and Gráinne Healy the organisation focused on establishing a strong policy unit and greater attention to women in poverty and the diversity of women's experiences of inequality. In 1998 Orla was asked by Katherine Zappone, the newly appointed CEO of NWCI, to represent NWCI on the European Social Fund Monitoring Committee, specifically focusing on employment, education and training initiatives. Subsequently, NWCI got significant funding from Atlantic Philanthropies, and a portion of that was to set up a policy unit. In 2000 a position came up as a policy officer, and Orla got her first job in NWCI. She would later go on to become head of policy.

After having her son Adam in 2010, Orla took a year off. As she returned to NWCI there was a "huge crisis with a massive cut in funding" due to the policies of austerity, which hit the community and voluntary sector. This would bring about, she said, a general crisis within the organisation in terms of future direction and priorities. Orla was asked to be acting CEO. She later applied for that position when it was advertised and was appointed, but with the new title of director of NWCI.

Over the years she developed a high media profile promoting NWCI issues, and led a number of successful campaigns on a range of issues on women's rights, including social welfare reform, pension reform and the introduction of quality and affordable childcare.

But when it came to abortion her memory is that within NWCI there was a real "nervousness" around the issue and how to deal with it. There were very different views on the subject:

> "My experiences at that time certainly did help me for the future in terms of understanding that people will have diverse views and often conflicting views on abortion. I really did understand that this was a hugely difficult issue for women. They were really uncomfortable even talking about it. There were strong differences of opinion and this would often silence others. I learned how important it was to create safe spaces around difficult issues."

That nervousness was exacerbated by a previous controversial referendum, unrelated to abortion, on Irish citizenship. Held in 2004, there had been considerable scaremongering around this time about immigration, frequently targeted at pregnant migrant women. NWCI called on all women to vote No in the referendum, arguing that the proposal was discriminatory and contrary to the values of a society that aspired to be equal and just, and where the ideal of cherishing all the children of the nation equally was enshrined in the constitution. However, the vote showed almost 80 per cent of people supported ending the automatic right to citizenship at birth of Irish-born children of immigrants. Afterwards, NWCI was questioned on its representative mandate:

> "So mandate was a very big issue for me when it came to abortion. I knew that at each stage there has to be ownership from the members and we could only do that by creating the spaces to bring people together on what was considered as one of the most difficult issues for women's rights in Ireland. If it went wrong there were enormous implications for women in

Ireland, for when abortion would be put back on the political agenda again and also for the future of NWCI."

Gráinne Griffin, the least publicly known of the three women, was born in London to Irish parents. Her family – she is one of five siblings and has a twin sister, Jessie – moved home to Ireland when she was a young child.

Gráinne went to the Ursuline Convent secondary school in Waterford, where she first became involved in human rights campaigning through the school's Peace and Justice Group. She remembers being really struck as a teenager by President Mary Robinson when she visited the school and spoke on the political nature of access to water globally. In primary school she was in the first group of altar girls in the parish – a situation that came about after she and friends had objected to boys being the only ones allowed to serve Mass.

Gráinne moved to Dublin for college in UCD in 2002, where she studied Social Science, and remembered that time as when she first became politically aware and directly involved in activism:

"I loved university. I was incredibly active and got very involved in campaigning around issues like the deportation of asylum seekers in Direct Provision, the Coca-Cola boycott, and the war in Iraq. I also worked very hard on the Shell to Sea campaign in Rossport, organising in the Dublin branch of that campaign. I found a strong connection between activism and academia, studying Irish Social Policy and Sociology in a time of rapid social change."

The issue of immigration and working with asylum seekers, she said, allowed critical engagement with the academic material and provided her with a grounding in theory. It also led to her working on that 2004 referendum that asked voters to remove the automatic entitlement of all those born in Ireland to citizenship at birth.

Marino Branch
Brainse Marino
Tel: 8336297

"I was 20 then and I campaigned for a No vote and learnt a lot of lessons on referendums", said Gráinne:

> "I suppose they're all things that matter to me. I'm an organiser and active and I fell into it quite naturally. And since there was a strong social aspect I made very good lifelong friends. I also learned a huge amount from it all, and brought a lot of that into the workforce later, in terms of organising skills."

After graduating from college in 2006, Gráinne became very active for a number of years in organising a successful and energetic social centre in Dublin city called Seomra Spraoi. She described it as an autonomous social space. Based on the tradition of social centres around Europe, Seomra Spraoi had various locations around the city, the final one being just off Mountjoy Square. The idea, said Gráinne, was to create the kind of world that you want to live in:

> "There were kitchens, cafe nights, cinema nights, free English classes; parents set up a Waldorf Steiner crèche upstairs; there were meetings for all, and every type of group. We ran fundraiser gigs to pay the rent. Every radical activist campaign in Dublin met there at some point. It brought everyone together and was a brilliant way to organise and to meet people. It was really practical and as a method of organising I found it particularly suited women. It operated on a consensus model so it was fantastic training in terms of dispute resolution, organising volunteers, participating in meetings, management, facilitation and logistics. We had a bike workshop at the back open to the public. We built a politically aware, compassionate and fun community. Towards the end of that time I also became involved in the Workers Solidarity Movement."

But in 2012, as the Abortion Rights Campaign (ARC) began to form, Gráinne made a decision that she was going to concentrate her volunteer time exclusively on abortion rights for Irish women. She believed then that nothing would change unless the issue was pushed to the top of the social and political agenda. Gráinne had previously been sporadically involved in pro-choice activism while at university, but it had never been the primary focus of her activism. One of the first times Gráinne was directly confronted with the reality of abortion access in Ireland was prior to the formation of ARC. A woman asked her to help somebody import abortion pills via the North. She didn't know the woman well; in fact she had only met her once at an activist training event. She was a friend of a friend. During one workshop Gráinne minded her little girl while her mother attended. A few months later she got a call from that woman out of the blue saying she was pregnant and was trying to access an abortion. She knew Gráinne was pro-choice and had contacts in the North.

"She did that thing that women often do and that she clearly felt she needed to do, of explaining just why she couldn't go ahead with the pregnancy. She told me she needed to get abortion pills and get them posted to the North and would I be able to help her? And of course I did. But I remember being just so struck by the fact that she had needed to resort to ringing me. She was very well-educated, middle class; every attribute you could think of that might help her navigate the situation. She didn't know me; she had to get my number from somebody and then ring me up, on the advice of a mutual friend, to ask me to help her import abortion pills. It was such a degrading position for her to be put in. I was horrified.

Abortion was one of those things people would become active on when it came up in the headlines; I remember being outside the High Court in 2007 for the Miss D case. There were some notable activists who did try and keep it on the agenda like Choice Ireland. I would attend their pickets of rogue pregnancy advisory clinics, run by the anti-abortion side, to intimidate and prevent women from traveling to the UK. There was no sense then of public or political support for a referendum; even the regulation of rogue clinics and the introduction of X Case legislation seemed very unlikely. ... I found that public activism on social issues moved from topic to topic, reacting to public events such as the bin tax or the Iraq War; it was a list of causes that just keep going like a hamster on a wheel. Campaigning generally involved countless meetings with the same group, of men mainly, who knew each other very well, and that dynamic wasn't going to change. So while everyone was sympathetic to abortion rights, I knew that until it was prioritised and people put their shoulder to the wheel consistently, we weren't going to get anywhere with it."

It was in 2012 that Gráinne decided that she would step back from her other commitments and prioritise the issue for seven years, because that is the time she calculated it would take to bring about and win a referendum to repeal the Eighth Amendment to the Constitution.

So between the three of them these women separately realised that only a huge effort would make a referendum on abortion happen in the first place and then to ensure that it was a victory.

2

The Most Shameful of Secrets

~~~~~~

Putting a face to a name when discussing an actual experience of abortion in Ireland was an absolute rarity. This was despite the fact there were almost 170,000 Irish women who underwent that procedure from 1980 to 2016 in the UK, according to statistics from their Department of Health. However that figure is an under-estimation of the overall number; many women who travelled from Ireland over those years would have given UK addresses, while some would have travelled to other countries such as The Netherlands, although in far smaller numbers, and in later years women would have increasingly used the abortion pill, ordered online, to terminate their pregnancies.

For reasons of secrecy and shame women simply kept it to themselves. But even, for instance, if each one had told just one other person that meant that hundreds of thousands of members of the Irish population had been directly or indirectly involved in the experience of abortion.

We often heard from the clergy or from politicians or the legal profession on the vexed issue of abortion in Irish society, but the space for the personal testimony of women who had actually undergone the experience was never filled, not in public and frequently, as we learned, not even privately among family and friends. It was always treated as the most shameful of secrets, not for discussion, often taken to the deathbed.

In 1983 Irish journalist Mary Holland wrote of her own abortion. At the time she was the subject of stinging criticism and received hate mail. But her revelation did not pave the way for others to tell their stories. Well over a decade later, in 1995, she returned to the subject, writing in the wake of the 1992 X Case: "It would be an enormous relief if some younger woman or women were to start writing about the issue of abortion from personal experience and leave me to the relatively easy task of analysing the peace process. Please", she wrote in the *Irish Times*.

The X Case was the real scar on the Irish abortion landscape, one of the most controversial legal battles in the history of the State, with that High Court decision preventing a fourteen-year-old girl from travelling abroad for an abortion.

The phrase 'to travel' was a well-known one in the Irish lexicon, a constant fact but one rarely spoken about in the open. However people had begun to join the dots in the 2000s in terms of linking the abuse of women in mother and baby homes (institutions run by nuns where young unmarried women were sent to have their babies), the incarceration of women in Magdalene laundries, and the appalling treatment of children in industrial schools and orphanages, as well as sexual abuse by priests in the Catholic Church.

The Irish political establishment was quite happy to keep the troublesome issue of abortion under wraps for as long as it possibly could. But as had been the cyclical way of this matter in Irish life, abortion had been just about due for further airing when a judgment came in on a case against Ireland. In 2010, the European Court of Human Rights in Strasbourg found the State had violated the rights of a woman who had cancer who said she was forced to travel abroad to get an abortion. This put abortion right back on the agenda. At that time pro-choice groups said the Government had little option except to introduce legislation or clear guidelines to provide for this type of lawful abortion. The anti-abortion side argued it was under no such obligation and called for a fresh referendum on the issue. Then Taoiseach Brian Cowen said the ruling in that *A, B and C v Ireland* case raised "difficult issues" that needed to be carefully considered.

Then in April 2012 something unheard of in the Irish abortion landscape happened. The names and faces of Irish women who had had abortions appeared in a newspaper. Journalist Kathy Sheridan had invited women to contact the *Irish Times* to share their experiences of abortion. A number of these turned out to be women who had received a diagnosis of fatal foetal abnormality (FFA) when they were pregnant, and deciding on a termination had to travel outside of Ireland for it. Some of these interviews took place in the NWCI offices. The women and their partners were very nervous around how their experiences would be perceived, but they wanted their stories heard.

At that time in the Dáil, publicly airing the matter further, a private members' bill to give effect to the 20-year-old Supreme Court decision in the *X* Case was introduced by independent TD Clare Daly on behalf of herself, Deputy Joan Collins of People Before Profit and independent TD Mick Wallace. The Medical Treatment (Termination of Pregnancy in Case of Risk to Life of Pregnant Woman) legislation in 2012 would have allowed for abortion where there was a real and substantial risk to the life of the mother. The Government defeated the bill by 101 votes to 27 with the support of Fianna Fáil.

Elsewhere, a fourteen-member expert group was studying the options on how to implement that earlier European Court of Human Rights ruling. In an initial article on abortion in February 2012, journalist Kathy Sheridan wondered about the motives, experiences and outcomes for women who travelled for terminations. She invited other people to share their experiences with the newspaper.

Years later Sheridan would say that her enduring memory of those ground-breaking pages that would subsequently be published, of Irish women's experiences of abortion, was the "raw terror" of the women revealing their names to her, solely for verification, not publication.

Out of that group who had had a diagnosis of a fatal foetal anomaly emerged four women who made social history when they were photographed and named on the front of the *Irish Times* on 17 April 2012 – Ruth Bowie, Amanda Mellet, Arlette Lyons and Jenny McDonald. They spoke of having to travel abroad for abortions after developing pregnancies with FFA and how they felt "ignored and stigmatised" by health services in Ireland. Their stories resulted in a huge public sympathy.

Orla O'Connor remembers her interactions with these couples who would go on to form the group Terminations for Medical Reasons (TFMR). They asked her to chair a briefing of Oireachtas members, between themselves and TDs and senators in Leinster House. Orla was only in the position of acting NWCI CEO for a few months at that time, but she remembers it as being a pivotal experience:

"I was chairing the meeting and I was getting really upset at their stories, their courage. There were two couples and five women who gave powerful testimony about their experiences of having to go abroad for an abortion after they had been told their pregnancies were diagnosed with fatal foetal abnormalities. It was so emotional and difficult, not least that they were also challenged at the time by anti-choice Oireachtas members."

After that meeting Orla remembers very clearly saying to herself that as NWCI director she would put every effort into working on the abortion issue in Ireland. Founded in 1973, NWCI takes its mandate from its over 190 member groups and individuals from across a diversity of backgrounds and sectors located throughout Ireland. As a result, policy and positions on abortion are membership-driven. During the previous decade members proposed and agreed motions on abortion, and at the 2009 AGM the membership voted for NWCI to develop a policy on safe and legal abortion. This pro-choice mandate, explained Orla, called for the provision of safe, legal abortion for women in this State and was rooted in an analysis of gender equality, women's human rights and social inclusion.

In May 2012, in light of the anniversary of the X Case, NWCI established a working group of members to look at legislation surrounding that case and to set down a policy for safe and legal abortion in Ireland. Earlier that year a members' meeting was held, 'From X to ABC: 20 Years of Inaction on Reproductive Rights'.

That summer the abortion temperature rose again when Youth Defence, the anti-abortion group, ran an advertising campaign on billboards, at train stations and with free-standing ads. It used the slogan 'Abortion Tears Her Life Apart' alongside a torn photograph of a distressed young woman, and a further tagline, 'There's always a better answer'. A second ad had a torn photograph of an ultrasound scan where the foetus was sucking its thumb. The campaign caused a storm of complaints at the time.

"People were going to Tesco and they were faced with a billboard of a foetal scan ripped in half saying 'Abortion tears her life apart'", remembered Gráinne Griffin. "I knew women who had never been involved in anything before and they were compelled to act by this." Sinéad Kennedy, who worked closely for years with Ailbhe Smyth campaigning on abortion rights, also remembered how those incendiary ads "galvanised a whole new layer of women". She recalled how Sinéad Redmond, who would subsequently become a colleague of hers in Maynooth University, set up a Facebook page in response to this with the lengthy but pointed title: 'Unlike Youth Defence I trust women to decide their lives for themselves'. "That page got loads and loads of likes and people saying something had to be done about this", recalled Sinéad Kennedy.

Just six months later a woman's name would become known worldwide in the most tragic of circumstances when Savita Halappanavar (31) died following a septic miscarriage in October 2012 in University Hospital Galway. The Indian woman, who had moved to Ireland with her husband, Praveen, attended the gynaecology unit at UHG at seventeen weeks pregnant and was subsequently told she was miscarrying. She was later admitted and as time went on she became increasingly distressed and was in terrible pain. However her request for a medical termination was refused. The couple was told at one point that this was because Ireland was a Catholic country and a foetal heartbeat was still present. Savita died of sepsis a week after she was admitted.

The headline on the front of the *Irish Times*, on 14 November 2012, over an article by Kitty Holland, declared: 'Woman "denied a termination" dies in hospital'. The story beneath told of the death two weeks previously of Savita. Savita's death meant abortion once again exploded into our public debate and put the international spotlight on Irish abortion laws. The *India Times* covered the story with the headline 'Ireland murders pregnant Indian dentist', while for the *New York Times* it was 'Hospital Death in Ireland Renews Fight Over Abortion'.

The reaction at home was swift. Appalling as the X Case had been, it did not involve a death and it pre-dated the 24/7 news cycle and social media, where on this occasion people flocked to express their dismay.

The anger spilled onto the streets. Candlelit vigils took place all over the country. Those who may have felt a slight ambivalence, or a desire to not become involved in the debate, felt compelled to express their anger publicly that in modern-day Ireland a woman died because her pregnancy had not been terminated.

On that Wednesday night after the story broke, thousands of people gathered in silent vigil outside the Irish parliament, Leinster House, holding candles. On the Saturday around 20,000 people marched in Dublin, with simultaneous demonstrations across the country, chanting "Never again". Ailbhe and Orla spoke at the vigil in Dublin.

The activists behind the Abortion Rights Campaign (ARC), who had started setting up their new campaign in July 2012, had held the first March for Choice in Dublin only a few weeks previously, and were gearing themselves up for the X Case anniversary when news of Savita's death became known. As Gráinne remembered:

> "We were organising for the march and vigils in Dublin which were absolutely huge; people who had never been on a march before felt the need to come out and say 'no, this should not have happened and it cannot happen again.' And people organised vigils all over the country. We were just heartbroken at what had happened to Savita; all of our drive and hope for change and we were too late for her, we'd failed her."

In the aftermath of Savita's death, Orla felt it was clear the mood was shifting in Ireland and a great willingness to discuss abortion was emerging. This was coupled with the considerable work NWCI had done on the issue that year. At that time NWCI called for a number of abortion-related changes: the repeal of the provisions of the Offences Against the Person Act 1861 in relation to abortion, and immediate legislation to implement the Supreme Court ruling in the X Case and the 2010 judgment of the European Court of Human Rights in the A, B and C v Ireland case. "There was such outrage about Savita's death at that time. There was a momentum from our membership that NWCI leadership was needed to generate a national discussion", said Orla.

NWCI wanted to do something different so it launched an e-action campaign. This was a digital tool that was developed so people could log onto the website, locate themselves, see who their local TDs were, and then send a direct email to those TDs. As Orla explained:

> "The email spoke about Savita and then it said Ireland needed to have a referendum to repeal the Eighth Amendment. In the end there were over 72,000 emails sent. I remember politicians in

the Dáil, and particularly Fine Gael and Fianna Fáil politicians, coming to us and saying they'd never seen anything like this. To have women and men constituents contacting them directly asking for legislation on abortion. It was also the first time we had men phoning into the Women's Council saying 'how can we help?'. Initially we didn't know how to harness it and then we started the online campaign. The fact that TDs were getting individual emails from constituents made a big difference."

Up to this, politicians would almost exclusively have been used to receiving correspondence from the anti-abortion side of the debate, so this e-action marked a new turn in the fight, where elected representatives now found themselves strongly lobbied on both sides. Ailbhe Smyth remembered the galvanising effect of Savita's death. It was very clear, she said, to those who had been working on the issue for a very long time that this was the moment to make a push. Around the time of the economic crash, she said, feminist groups, including Feminist Open Forum and the Irish Feminist Network, had been set up and were increasingly active and visible.

"People were appalled and from that moment on they began to think 'there is something not right here, I don't like this', and this meant there was a conflict for them, because people here are conditioned to see abortion as morally wrong, which comes from being raised a Catholic in a very narrow frame of reference. But then there was a sense of shame at the terrible tragedy that had befallen a young woman having her first baby who was in a vulnerable situation because she had come here from elsewhere to work with her young husband. It was as if she had been rejected by us on every level. It showed people there was no flexibility in our system, and no flexibility means no kindness, no compassion, no human understanding – that it didn't matter how bad a situation was, the law is the law, and the rules were the rules. People's hearts were opened by Savita and we had to push open the door after that."

The establishment of the Abortion Rights Campaign was certainly well-timed. Unsurprisingly perhaps, ARC had developed as a result of a call to pro-choice activism from the Dublin-based Revolutionary Anarcha-Feminist Group (RAG). Gráinne Griffin described RAG as a fabulous organisation of incredibly strong women who, among other things, published six issues of a female-authored magazine, *The RAG.* In July 2012 Marianne Farrelly and Angela Coraccio called a meeting of people interested in getting more organised about abortion, in the social centre Seomra Spraoi. There were about 40 people in attendance. From that meeting the Irish Choice Network, then to become the Abortion Rights Campaign, was set up. True to form, the final name of the organisation would involve a huge amount of discussion and was decided by the members through an online poll. The Abortion Rights Campaign was not just a name; it was an exercise in breaking down stigma because at that time it was quite provocative to have the word 'abortion' in the title. "You just didn't say the word out loud then. Some activists had argued for a softer name, focused on choice or women. That's really hard to explain to younger activists, that you just didn't say the word 'abortion' before Savita", recalls Gráinne. "Our primary goals were Repeal of the Eighth Amendment and to make abortion free, safe and legal to those who needed it."

They quickly started planning the set-up of a national grassroots campaign and also organised that first March for Choice, to coincide with International Safe Abortion Day on 28 September 2012. The day was first celebrated as a day of action for decriminalisation of abortion in Latin America and the Caribbean in 1990. There was a core group of around 30 individuals involved in ARC and one of their goals, said Gráinne, was to do everything to the absolute best of their abilities, aspiring to meet professional standards wherever possible. As Gráinne explained:

"A number of all-day facilitated meetings hammered out what the principles and objectives of our new organisation would be – the values, the strategy. There were discussions about campaign principles and objectives, where should we go and

> what we should ask for. There was definitely a sense from some older feminists and others pro-choice activists in Dublin that we were naïve and asking for far too much, that we didn't understand the reality that there would never be a referendum on broad access to abortion in Ireland. That we needed to understand that X Case legislation was the only realistic campaign objective and we should focus on that. These same activists were supportive of broader access but had been through decades of campaigning (and losing) and by then were so often tired and burnt out."

ARC launched its campaign publicly in January 2013 with a day of workshops in the Teachers' Club in Parnell Square in Dublin. The structure they opted for was fascinating and, as Gráinne says herself, quite bureaucratic. This is an organisation with no one in charge. She explained that this approach borrowed strongly from the anarchist principles of non-hierarchical organising:

> "The structure and all of the principles of the campaign were based on democratic, transparent, horizontal organising. It's a very tightly defined, completely democratic organisational system. It's leaderless by design, there was no – and people have difficulty with this – fixed leader of ARC. There was never going to be a chairperson. Each member has the same value and the same voice. Leadership positions of course exist but they rotate and are driven by a mandate. An ARC representative is always a delegate speaking for the wider organisation. That's the essential difference between that and parliamentary democracy, where someone is elected but relatively free to direct their own activity and positions, driven largely by their own political ideals. In horizontal organising it is all mandate-based."

The other key decision ARC made, drawing on its members' collective organising experience, was to embrace a wide range of tactics, not just what people would see as the traditional activist-based approaches of marching and banners. It was everything from well-researched policy work, such as preparing thorough submissions for the United Nations, outreach and collaboration with other groups, to a large and successful social media presence, active press work, and organising art exhibitions and public events, with everything presented with clever, high-quality graphic design and printing. "We decided that we would approach everything in as much as we could in a professional campaign and not lower our standards because we were volunteer-based. Being volunteer-based itself is also a core principle, so there were no paid staff."

Gráinne acknowledged this approach and the task at hand involved a major time commitment for her, usually a couple of evenings a week:

> "The idea was that everybody who wanted to contribute would find a place depending on what they wanted to work on and how much time they had to give. So if you were creative or an artist, or wanted to do a performance-based piece on the street, there was a creative actions group. But if you were coming from a political or policy background, or you were a lawyer, or a student lawyer, there was a policy and advocacy group where you could research and contribute to policy formation and submissions."

There were a number of working groups and two delegates from each working group and regional group would attend the monthly ARC steering group meeting. The campaign as a whole elected two co-convenors who ran the campaign. The co-convenors, along with the treasurer and the secretary, didn't have a vote on the steering group. So the core secretariat was non-voting and all of the people who came from the working groups had a mandate.

> "So yes it can appear as a convoluted structure. If you're used to an NGO with a chairperson and a CEO, it's very different to that. People did sometimes find it hard to get involved; different people have different expectations and desires of what they want from a volunteer organisation group. Some people would

prefer to be told what to do. ARC relies on initiative and drive and members bringing something to the table. You feel 'I'm doing work.' It's not a talking shop. There was always a difficulty explaining the structure. But over the years hundreds of amazing people came in to ARC and got active and gave time, and where it worked, it worked brilliantly, really, really effectively."

People looking in did find it puzzling how such a group could work, or indeed the value of spending hours on discussion in order to work through issues. It sometimes made it difficult to build alliances. ARC was certainly good at fundraising and members were prepared to work hard to raise money. It was one of the few campaigning groups at the time with the resources to rent an office. The group sold merchandise from the start – T-shirts, badges and stickers – all with what would have then been viewed as the uncompromising slogan 'Free Safe Legal' on them.

The first campaign ARC ran was a tourist-style postcard campaign, printing 30,000 high-quality colour cards, which at the time seemed a huge volume, that said, in retro typeface: "Welcome to Ireland, failing to take action on abortion since 1992" along-side the slogan "Legislate for X". The group encouraged people to send the postcards to politicians. On a steep learning curve, they organised press conferences and photo shoots. There was lots of banner-making, placards and different art events.

But even with their hard work and meticulous preparations, and the relationship building through the work on submissions to the United Nations with other groups, Gráinne was aware that a certain perception of ARC as 'studenty' would always remain. "We were fringe; we were outside of the NGO scene so to speak", recalled Gráinne:

"We were not identified as leaders or particularly important at that stage even though many would fall over themselves now to say that they were always cognisant of how important we were. It wasn't easy to get a volunteer organisation to the policy table. People in Ireland like to know who's in charge, they want to build relationships. But our campaign representatives changed on an annual basis at our AGM, so people and organisations would build a relationship with a convenor over a year and then they had two other new women to work with. But it was brilliant for developing young women leaders up through the organisation and supporting their entry into positions sometimes before even they knew they were ready. A year later, they would leave the role confident, capable and ready to coach two new women who had been elected as co-convenors."

Gráinne acknowledged that ARC's system of working has its disadvantages but argued that any negatives are far outweighed by the positives.

"It really was an organisation of incredibly strong, capable women. One of the wonderful things to watch over the years was members' progression and success in their professional and other lives, clearly building on skills and confidence developed within ARC."

Sarah Monaghan, another ARC member, who worked closely with Gráinne, is equally enthusiastic about the method of operating and agreed that she could not imagine an all-male group operating similarly:

"Honestly I just can't. Given my experience in the sector, and thinking of groups we may have worked with over the years, I can't imagine it happening. The people who ask the most questions about the structure, in terms of minimising us, are always men. They view it as massively ineffective time-wasting, that we were operating in this way because we were all a bit unsure. Instead of it being a very well-thought-out, highly complex structure and in fact a much more difficult way to do it. Normal hierarchical structures come with a lot of comfort; leading with full communication and transparency with all of your membership, and with a large membership – that is extremely difficult."

3

Keeping Repeal on the Agenda

~~~~~~~~~~~~~~~~~~~~~~~~~~~~~~~~

Following Savita's death, Ailbhe Smyth and Sinéad Kennedy, a long-time activist and campaigner on abortion, strongly believed that a timeframe was needed on the holding of an abortion referendum. In Ailbhe's mind it would be done within five years. It was going to be a tough battle and involve serious work and cooperation where, in some cases, none had previously existed. Those years were ones of bringing people together, intensive lobbying, strategising and defining the issue in the political and public mind, all the while mobilising a support base increasingly restless for action. During that time relationships between the various groups and individuals were solidified around a common goal: repeal of the Eighth Amendment.

As soon as the Protection of Life During Pregnancy Act (PLDPA) became law in 2013, Ailbhe approached Orla O'Connor and said she intended setting up a coalition of groups to repeal the Eighth Amendment and did NWCI wish to be a part of that. The NWCI board, led by Chairperson Siobhán O'Donoghue, was very supportive and very clear on the mandate of the organisation to pursue a liberalisation of the abortion laws. Orla and Jacqueline Healy, who was then NWCI women's health officer, had been working internally to increase the focus on abortion in the work of NWCI. Orla explains:

"I felt we needed to be more publicly visible and active on women's reproductive rights. So we developed an abortion policy and then circulated it to the full membership for consultation. It was very clear and very public and it was agreed by the membership. There were some members who said, 'I don't agree fully with this', but they also said, 'I understand why you're doing this', and no member left as a result. And that was really important because when we had a policy and a clear mandate then we could start to publicly campaign. That was a significant moment because NWCI, as the national women's organisation, viewed by many as a mainstream organisation, putting Repeal and access to abortion at the centre of our agenda became a talking point. We quickly got media attention for what we were saying. It was the first time we started to articulate what free, safe and legal meant in terms of abortion access. And we backed it up by international evidence."

At that time in the Coalition Government the junior partner, the Labour Party, was in favour of repealing the Eighth Amendment but the larger party, Fine Gael, was significantly divided on the issue. The then party leader and Taoiseach, Enda Kenny, gave all the appearances of someone who would prefer never to have to deal with the issue of abortion. But he had to contend with the public outcry after the death of Savita Halappanavar, and that landmark 2010 European Court of Human Rights judgment. There was also the pressure to finally give legislative effect to the 1992 Supreme Court ruling in the X Case. It was in light of all of this that the Protection of Life During Pregnancy Act (PLDPA) was introduced. This legislation would prove politically tumultuous in many respects. Significantly, the run-up to the legislation was the first time that two of the masters of the Dublin maternity hospitals, Dr Rhona Mahony of the National Maternity Hospital and Dr Sam Coulter-Smith of the Rotunda, as well as campaigning groups, including NWCI and Action on X, all presented to the Joint Oireachtas Committee on Health. Issues surrounding abortion, and the experiences of women forced to travel, were finally being debated in the Oireachtas. The bill resulted in the loss of six TDs in Fine Gael who were expelled from the parliamentary party over their opposition to the legislation.

The 30th anniversary of the signing into law of the Eighth Amendment to the Constitution, another significant anniversary in the abortion wars, was due to fall on 7 October 2013, and had been a focus for Repeal campaigners. In the event, the PLDPA legislation was put on the statute books just ahead of the anniversary. So by then the discussion was no longer centred on whether we could have abortion in Ireland, but rather in what circumstances it could be allowed. While it was a defeat for the anti-abortion lobby, which had fought the Act tenaciously, the abortion law was also the most restrictive in Europe at that time. It provided for access to abortion only where a pregnant woman or girl's life, as distinct from her health, was at risk. It criminalised any woman, or girl, who procured an abortion outside the confines of the legislation, punishing her and anyone who assisted her with up to fourteen years in prison.

It did not allow for abortion where a woman was pregnant as a result of rape or incest or where she was carrying a foetus with a fatal abnormality. It differentiated between a physical and a mental threat to a woman's life, and compelled the woman, if suicidal, to submit to assessment by up to six doctors.

For its part, the Abortion Rights Campaign had decided to call for a No vote by politicians on the legislation, particularly incensed at the threat of fourteen years in prison. This decision was made after discussion and with the knowledge, said Gráinne, that women in Ireland were accessing the abortion pill illegally and genuinely were in danger of facing a prison sentence. The 'abortion pill' is the common name for using two different medicines – mifepristone and misoprostol – to end a pregnancy. A mifepristone pill is taken first. Then the misoprostol is taken either immediately, or up to 48 hours later. The medicine can cause cramping and heavy bleeding. It was a game-changer in terms of a majority of women in early pregnancy not needing a surgical abortion. However, in other countries the process would be medically supervised, unlike in Ireland where it was illegal. As Gráinne outlined:

"I think it was a critical decision for us, in terms of learning to stand on our principles. It was doubtful if the State would have prosecuted a woman under the 1861 Act, but a newly enacted law that clearly set out a fourteen-year sentence, that was a different story. In the end, Clare Daly and a couple of other TDs did vote No on the basis that it wasn't fit for purpose; it would do more harm than good."

Orla said NWCI viewed the passing of the bill strategically as a first step towards access to abortion. For her part, Ailbhe described the PLDPA as window-dressing but also had a pragmatic view on it as an opening that could be used to gather support for the repeal of the Eighth Amendment. At that time she was part of a group called Action on X, set up around the twentieth anniversary of the X Case, which subsequently became Action for Choice. She recalled that a group of around twenty people had got together to try to make the PLDPA legislation as strong as possible. That meant overcoming their own misgivings in order to get a piece of legislation onto the statute books that recognised the X Case Supreme Court judgment. As Ailbhe recalled:

"Politics is always the art of compromise and pragmatism. So the Government of the day had, as far as they were concerned,

> behaved very politically and strategically and said 'Right we
> will shut this one down with a piece of nonsense legislation, and
> we'll be home and dry for a while with that.' But at the same
> time we were thinking 'you're dead wrong about that', and
> being strategic. We saw there was now an opening, a breach.
> We had a way in now and we were going to keep it on the
> agenda. We knew there would be a general election at some
> stage and we had to get in there on the general election tickets
> so to speak."

Looking around her, Ailbhe said she recognised that a number of individuals and groups were active in the same space, and had been for
years, but operating in their own silos. There were others who were
well-disposed to the Repeal argument but hadn't been active on it:

> "I talked a lot with Sinéad Kennedy about what we needed
> to do. I was very clear: we needed to bring people together
> somehow; that meant the usual suspects – pro-choice and
> feminist groups and organisations – and the people who had
> never been suspected at all, but who would have an interest, a
> stake in it, such as the trade unions. We had to put Repeal on the
> agenda."

So in September 2013 she and Sinéad set about doing that with the
aim of extending beyond the traditional pro-choice organisations to
build a national platform of organisations across civil society, trade
unions and political parties calling for Repeal. Naming it as a constitutional issue was deliberate and strategic. The aim was to re-position
the issue of abortion; to set constitutional change as a fundamental
and achievable first step towards obtaining the provision of abortion
in Ireland. It was also to draw in groups and organisations that
did not necessarily have an explicit pro-choice policy. In coming
together the key players would all have an understanding of what
needed to be done to be successful in bringing about this change.
But this also involved considerable consensus-building. Given the
broad spectrum of groups and views involved this was inevitably

challenging. As time went on the Coalition to Repeal the Eighth Amendment would become a strategic driver, putting shape and narrative around a broad Repeal movement.

The Coalition to Repeal the Eighth Amendment came together formally with twelve organisations: NWCI, ARC, AkiDwA (a network of migrant women living in Ireland), the Union of Students in Ireland, Cork Women's Right to Choose, Terminations for Medical Reasons, Doctors for Choice, the Dublin Well Woman Centre, the Irish Council for Civil Liberties, People Before Profit, the Socialist Party, and the trade union Unite.

On the 30th anniversary of the signing of the Eighth Amendment to the Constitution, 7 October 2013, the group issued a joint statement to the media stating that they were twelve women's and civil society organisations wishing to highlight the detrimental impact of Article 40.3.3. It said the amendment was a mistake, continued to be a mistake and was a source of confusion and discrimination for women in this country. The statement concluded by calling on like-minded individuals and organisations to join this group to work for Repeal "and in doing so protect the lives and health of women and girls in Ireland."

Sinéad Kennedy said Ailbhe was the one person with the patience to make sure that it all worked. "We started with twelve organisations and then grew to be over 100. And that was largely down to Ailbhe and her charm and charisma. We work well together but she has that personality, that ability to bring people along. I have less patience with the kind of charm and cajoling that's involved. She's much better at that."

Leading up to this Orla remembered the conversations within NWCI and its over 180 member groups and how those discussions crystallised into the need to call for a referendum to repeal the Eighth Amendment:

"It was our experience that the Government was doing everything to avoid dealing with abortion. Whenever there was a public opportunity I would point out the absence of political leadership, the hypocrisy of our politicians burying their heads in the sand while women travelled and ignoring the risk to women's lives and health".

She was conscious of picking key events and moments to get that message across, and noticed that when NWCI spoke on the issue of abortion it tended to get noticed. The more open approach did not go unquestioned though.

"We were using a lot of public platforms to constantly put it up there, to say: 'This is a key issue'. Because it was NWCI talking about abortion it got attention. Up to then we were not the organisation leading the way on abortion. So we picked key highly visible moments for NWCI and brought the attention back to Repeal and the damage that was being done to women by the Eighth. But we were constantly questioned by politicians and journalists as to whether the membership of NWCI wanted Repeal and access to abortion.

The journalists would ask me: 'So you're saying NWCI and all your 180 member groups agree with this?' I had to keep explaining our position, how it was arrived at and saying yes this is what women want. So then they would say 'hang on a second now, what about the Irish Countrywomen's Association, they don't necessarily have that view.' The answer, which was the answer right up to the referendum, which is the truth, is they may not hold that individual position but they have supported the collective NWCI view by staying members of NWCI."

But she remembered being nervous at times, and one particular time when their bigger member groups got in touch to say they were being contacted by their own members and anti-choice organisations and asked why they supported the NWCI stance on abortion. As Orla explained:

"They were being contacted by people on the anti-choice side/ pro-life side. Again people didn't leave, but they were very uncomfortable and they didn't want that public hit. So there was a nervousness and there were organisations who consistently abstained. There was only about three or four who came to the AGM to abstain so that that would be recorded. It was Labour Women, led by Senator Ivana Bacik, who consistently proposed motions to develop the policy position. After the Coalition to Repeal the Eighth Amendment was formed, Ailbhe would also propose motions at each AGM so there would be a motion affirming the position. ARC also joined NWCI which added to the strength of the position. This was all important as it reinforced the mandate. It was also clear that each year more and more members felt more strongly about the issue which gave me and the team more confidence in our campaigns and justified the emphasis on and prioritisation of abortion within the organisation."

While State funding for NWCI could be as high as 85 per cent during those years, due to the cuts enforced by the recession and austerity it hovered around 60 per cent during the next three years, meaning NWCI was in a financially precarious position.

There was part-funding from private foundation Atlantic Philanthropies and funding from member subscriptions. Without doubt NWCI prodding the Government on an issue Fine Gael clearly would rather was left alone brought risk, but Orla was firm then in her view of what NWCI's job was in terms of abortion. In the following years NWCI would continue to push for repeal and reproductive rights through various policies and initiatives:

"We knew we had to be very strategic around our approach to advancing abortion. And that's why it's so important for NWCI to have membership funding so there is an independent source of funding that can be put towards campaigns. But we're also very clear, and it is part of the conversations we've had going back years with the Department of Justice and Equality, that we're funded by the State to bring the views of Irish women to Government. So it's not to tell the Government they're doing a great job; it's to represent the reality of women's lives and the inequalities and discrimination women experience. That's why it was always important for us that abortion policy was led by women's experiences and women's needs. That followed all the way through in the campaign both in getting the referendum called and how the campaign was run. As Director that's always been a guiding principle for me for me in terms of the work we do, and what we say."

A key factor to the influence NWCI could exert on the subject is that abortion and reproductive rights was one issue amongst many for women which NWCI was advancing:

"The fact that NWCI focuses on the many inequalities and lack of rights for women in Ireland made a difference when it came to discussing the issue of abortion. I could be talking about the gender pay gap, violence against women, pensions to very diverse audiences and always refer to the discrimination of forcing women to travel to access a basic healthcare – abortion. It brought a new dimension to the debate on abortion. Similarly, the credibility and track record of NWCI on women's rights meant that people listened to us when we spoke of women's needs and abortion as healthcare."

It took time for the Coalition to Repeal the Eighth to establish itself and how it would operate. One decision to simplify matters was to decide on one vote per organisation. Prospective members were told there was no document to sign, that the Coalition would follow democratic principles and also would respect the diverse nature of the organisations within it. It would also "keep agreed strategic direction under review and revise as needed".

But as Ailbhe remembered it, quite remarkably given the subject at hand, and the incredibly high stakes, they never did vote on anything:

"It was fairly clear that if we'd voted you'd have the left going one way, and the moderates going another. If things were

> fraught we would agree to think about the issue and come back to it at the next meeting. Our strategy was to build a very strong coalition composed of a big cohort of organisations. It was organisational membership only. And that was about ensuring that different stakeholders in this worked together, and were equally determined, despite crossing a spectrum of views on abortion, that whatever else we thought, we absolutely agreed that the Eighth Amendment had to go."

Given our history, the years of argument, the oppression of women and the internalised shame, this job of holding the Coalition together, especially over an extended period of time, would look, on paper, to be almost impossible. Even the original line-up of twelve organisations extending from the 'Free, Safe, Legal' position of the Abortion Rights Campaign or Action for Choice, to other more nuanced positions such as that of Unite, the first Irish union to publicly support the Repeal cause. With an element of understatement Ailbhe described it thus: "It is certainly true that for the first couple of years we did have a spectrum of views."

Gráinne acknowledged that while ARC was a founding member and supportive of the Coalition from the beginning, the same broad alliance could not have developed through her organisation, and that many members had a jaundiced view of it as an initiative:

> "The Coalition brought a lot of people together under a necessarily vague banner. It needed somebody who could do that and deal with everyone individually, and Ailbhe was brilliant at that. Now a lot of people in ARC wouldn't have had much time for the Coalition – the work carried out wasn't always visible and the way of operating was very different from ARC; it was firmly led by Ailbhe and you just kind of had to go with it. That was how it worked. What Ailbhe did was build and manage a network of existing organisations around the common goal of Repeal. It was a different strategy to ARC's. We were building a grassroots movement of individuals. Ailbhe was trying to build alliances around a common ground and keep everybody together. Part

of the ARC strategy from the get-go was to hold our position on access to abortion for anyone who needed it. Holding that position was really important on two counts, because that approach would give the best possible access to women but also because we knew that by holding what was seen as a very radical line we could create a space within which other groups could take more progressive positions than they would have otherwise. In a way, that was part of the strategy of not pushing for a shared position on what should come after Repeal."

Meanwhile, ARC was busy developing public information campaigns and building a grassroots membership around the country. It was also using a unique fundraising method as a way to mobilise new members. In 2013 an extraordinary alliance came about between ARC and the Workers Beer Company (WBC), a UK trade union initiative that provides mass catering to bars at music festivals in the UK and Ireland.

At the end of that first summer ARC had raised over €20,000. ARC's fifth and most successful summer of volunteering was in 2017, when it brought 450 volunteers to 19 events in Ireland and the UK, raising €73,000. For ARC that opportunity grasped in 2013 meant, according to Gráinne, who was subsequently appointed to the WBC Irish management committee, "massive, life-changing" money was available to use for campaigning:

"It was an insane level of work. For the volunteer coordinators it was like working a second full-time job. We'd get hundreds of volunteers signing up. We'd build a database, assign shifts, organise buses to the venues and back, manage cancellations, supervise the volunteers and, of course, work behind the bars."

Just under two years after the death of Savita Halappanavar, in the summer of 2014, another migrant woman who was refused an abortion, despite saying that she was suicidal, would come to general attention and cause further public protest. It was a poor comfort to those who had protested against the newly enshrined Protection of

Life During Pregnancy Act. It had only come into effect the previous January, under which abortion was to be allowed in limited circumstances, and this woman was refused one. Known as Miss Y, the woman, who was not an Irish citizen, had arrived in the State as an asylum-seeker earlier that year and discovered she was pregnant shortly afterwards. She said she had been raped before she arrived in the country. At about eight weeks pregnant she made contact with crisis pregnancy services. She became increasingly distressed as it became clear she was unable to travel for an abortion due to the costs involved and restrictions on her right to travel.

After coming to the attention of Health Service Executive psychiatric services at about 24 weeks' gestation, it was deemed too late to abort the pregnancy, despite the fact she had been deemed suicidal under the provisions of the Protection of Life During Pregnancy Act (PLDPA). After her request for an abortion was rejected, the woman began a brief hunger strike, refusing food and liquids, but eventually agreed to a caesarean section after the HSE began legal proceedings to forcibly hydrate her. She gave birth to a baby boy at around 25 weeks' gestation.

After the story broke in the *Irish Independent* NWCI posted a message on Twitter saying that the refusal to permit an abortion in the case was "barbaric." Just weeks before that the chairman of the United Nations Human Rights Committee (UNHRC), Sir Nigel Rodley, said he was sorry the PLDPA did not extend to the right to the health of women. He made his remarks as the then Minister for Justice Frances Fitzgerald appeared before the UN Human Rights Committee in Geneva. Adding further embarrassment to the Irish Government, he said:

> "Life without quality of life is not something many of us have to choose between and to suggest that, regardless of the health consequences of a pregnancy, a person may be doomed to continue it at the risk of criminal penalty is difficult to understand. Even more so regarding rape when the person doesn't even bear any responsibility and is by the law clearly treated as a vessel and nothing more."

Minister Fitzgerald told the committee it would take another referendum to make abortion permissible on other grounds such as fatal foetal abnormalities. In 2015 the UN Committee on Economic, Social and Cultural Rights would report its concerns at Ireland's "highly restrictive legislation on abortion" and called for a referendum to repeal the Eighth Amendment. It all combined to build strong international pressure on the Government, including through the UN and the Council of Europe, to provide abortion in Ireland.

In reaction to Sir Nigel's remarks ARC began the #NotAVessel campaign on social media, which got a large response, with women posting photos of themselves with signs showing the hashtag, and directing their posts to Minister Fitzgerald and then Tánaiste and leader of the Labour Party, Joan Burton. ARC had previously submitted a report to the UNHRC International Covenant on Civil and Political Rights (ICCPR). Showing increasing levels of cooperation, ARC collaborated with other groups for the presentation in Geneva – the Irish Council for Civil Liberties (ICCL), the Irish Family Planning Association, Doctors for Choice, Terminations for Medical Reasons and the Centre for Reproductive Rights.

Ireland had been due to be examined by the UNHRC on how the State was complying with ICCPR and it was decided ARC would present a joint statement on Ireland's abortion laws to the UNHRC on behalf of a number of reproductive-rights-focused NGOs. The hard work and cooperation felt well worth it when Sir Nigel's strongly worded remarks brought such attention to the abortion regime in Ireland. As Gráinne recalled:

"We became experts in abortion. We studied the World Health Organisation papers on it and learnt what international best practice required. Because actually very few people in Ireland knew much about abortion policy. Certainly politicians were not well informed on it. It's not that complex an area, yet so few people were very well versed in it, both in terms of the human rights dialogue and just general reproductive health."

Towards the end of 2014 there was yet another case which appalled people, gained further international attention, and further raised the stakes on the need for a referendum. A young woman who was fifteen weeks pregnant was declared clinically dead at a Dublin hospital as a result of a brain trauma suffered at a hospital outside Dublin, two days after she had been admitted there complaining of severe headaches.

The tragedy played out in the courts over that Christmas. The doctors at the Dublin hospital where she was being treated were concerned they would be prosecuted if they ended life support because of the legal implications of her pregnancy, arising from the State's obligation to vindicate the right to life of the unborn in Article 40.3.3 – the 1983 amendment to the Constitution.

Her father, supported by her partner and extended family, had applied to the High Court for orders stopping treatment so they could bury her "with dignity". The court heard that a photograph of the woman was by her bed but she bore "not a whole lot of resemblance" to it. Make-up was applied to her face because her children came to see her, but the swelling of her eyes had gotten so bad that they did not close. The children found it distressing.

The woman, in her 20s and referred to in the media as Miss P, had an ongoing infection, presumed to be pneumonia. She appeared puffy, her blood pressure fluctuated and her abdomen showed signs of inflammation and discolouration. She had an open head wound and her brain appeared to the naked eye to be rotting. Blood flow to the brain had stopped.

Her father said she no longer looked like his daughter and the eldest of her two young children had been very distressed when she had seen her mother the previous week. On St Stephen's Day, when the woman was eighteen weeks pregnant, the High Court, in a landmark judgment, ruled that doctors could switch off the life support machine.

However, almost six months later there was an occasion for major celebration with the marriage equality referendum, held on 22 May 2015, allowing people of the same gender to marry. On the basis that referendums can only be fought one at a time, campaigning on abortion had to be low-profile at that stage for a number of people, particularly Ailbhe, who was on the executive group of the Yes Equality campaign. It was an amazing victory when Ireland officially passed the referendum with 1.2 million people voting in its favour, 62 per cent voting Yes and a large 60.5 per cent turnout.

There was a massive outpouring of love and joy around that successful referendum result and in its wake there was a great sense of possibility for an abortion referendum. In the shorter term it resulted in a considerable strengthening of the hand of the Repeal campaigners as they faced into a general election.

Sinéad Kennedy, co-founder of the Coalition to Repeal the Eighth Amendment, remembered talking with Ailbhe in the aftermath of the marriage equality referendum and worrying how some people imagined that an abortion referendum could be a "marriage equality mark II":

> "This campaign couldn't be that, although people did want it to be that. I suppose marriage equality had really captured that sense of love and hope and possibility. And of course it's Ireland: who doesn't love a wedding and falling in love? It was positioned that way – just because I'm straight I can get married and have love and a family. Why should you deny your sons and daughters, your friends, simply because they're attracted to somebody of the same sex? So it was this wonderful flowering of love and support and recognition. Abortion is not like that; no one says 'I want to have an abortion.'"

Taoiseach Enda Kenny, showing his usual consistency on abortion, moved to dampen expectations by saying the Government would not be rushed into considering these matters simply "because we have just had a referendum with a positive outcome". The issue of abortion was much more complex than same-sex marriage and he did not support "abortion on demand". There would be no referendum on any aspect of the laws regarding termination before the next general election.

But increasingly evident was the political reality of the emergence of a national social movement for the liberalisation of our abortion laws. In October 2015 a bus organised by ROSA, a reproductive rights group against oppression, sexism and austerity, travelled around the country, with the group saying it would make abortion pills available to women who needed them and calling for a referendum to repeal the Eighth Amendment. Women with unwanted pregnancies were offered the opportunity to access pills on the bus after completing a Skype consultation with doctors from the Dutch pro-choice group 'Women on Web'.

But then in November the chances of an abortion referendum became considerably stronger after the Taoiseach announced a citizen's convention to focus on the Eighth Amendment to be set up within six months of the general election if he was re-elected. He had come under pressure from senior members of his own party, who were convinced Fine Gael had to enter the forthcoming general election campaign with a clear strategy on the issue. Afterwards, unlike with the PLDPA, Fine Gael TDs would have a free vote in the Dáil. The move was seen as an effort to avoid a damaging split within the party in advance of the election. The junior coalition partner, the Labour Party, had said it would insist on an early referendum as a precondition to re-entering coalition with Fine Gael in the event of the post-election numbers adding up.

ARC's March for Choice in Dublin in 2015 would double in size compared to the previous year, with 10,000 participants, indicating the increased consciousness of the issue. The political world was feeling the pressure where the reality of abortion for Irish women continued to be felt on a daily basis, but was no longer hidden and unspoken. In August 2016 one Irish woman live-tweeted her journey to the UK to have an abortion, accompanied by a friend, turning the personal into the political. The women used the account @twowomentravel with a bio that read: "Two Women, one procedure, 48 hours away from home." Before leaving Ireland on the Saturday morning they tweeted at Enda Kenny: "Good morning all. Thanks for all of the messages of solidarity and support. Thanks to @EndaKennyTD we're about to hit the road."

Later in the day the women appeared to be at the clinic: "Now a waiting room, weighted by bated breaths. @EndaKennyTD we could be home by noon in another world." Sometime later we were told that the abortion had taken place and the patient was "out and safe", and that the two women had encountered other Irish women there for the same reason. In a series of 30 tweets the story unfolded, and they also posted ordinary photographs including an Aer Lingus plane on the tarmac at Dublin airport that morning, and later a bloodied sheet at the clinic. "Not the first or the last bleeding women about to face a long trek home" read the accompanying tweet. After leaving the clinic they stayed the night in a hotel. The account attracted huge attention and was picked up by the international media.

Afterwards in an interview with Emer O'Toole in *The Guardian*, the friend of the woman who had had the abortion, wishing to remain anonymous, said while planning the journey her friend decided she wanted something good to come from it for Irish women. She asked:

> "What's the alternative? Silence? Silence is breaking 12 Irish hearts a day. Silence is trapping migrant women in desperate situations, silence has the blood of Savita on its hands; silence is the shape of Miss Y's devastation. Silence has devastated the women and girls of Ireland, but now it's time to talk, and get real."

One of the major targets for the Coalition to Repeal the Eighth Amendment was that next general election and the candidates who would run in it. The other key campaigning organisations involved had similar approaches, but they had done enough cooperating and preparing over the previous few years so as not to overlap, and not to compete with one another. ARC had already created videos and tools to encourage voters to highlight abortion as a key policy for the local elections in 2014 and they built on this work, rolling out a nationwide 'Talk to your TD' campaign, providing supporters with a detailed information pack to help them have conversations on the doorsteps about abortion. Providing background briefings on the situation in Ireland, it also responded to common myths about abortion and suggested questions that supporters could ask their local candidates.

As that February 2016 election approached the lobbying intensified, with the aim of getting enough candidates to publicly commit to holding a referendum on repeal of the Eighth Amendment at a minimum, and moreover to women's right to choose. The Coalition asked election candidates to commit to the statement: "I support the holding of a referendum to repeal the Eighth Amendment". NWCI had its 'Breakthrough Manifesto for Women', a ten-point document which it asked general election candidates to sign and pledge to work towards if elected. Point 6 in that document stated: "If elected I will support reproductive rights and repeal of the Eighth Amendment by delivering a referendum to remove the Eighth Amendment from our Constitution and bring Ireland in line with international human rights standards."

This resulted in further questioning of the role of NWCI and why it was asking candidates to sign such a pledge. Some candidates did not want to sign their name to it. Others, although not many, Orla recalled – clearly after being contacted by constituents – came back to NWCI to say they wanted their name off the list. They would say they hadn't read the manifesto properly when they initially agreed to it. These public commitments made it far clearer which politicians were comfortable to be associated with the Repeal movement, while there was a clear pattern of reluctance from Fine Gael and Fianna Fáil politicians.

Ailbhe observes that in the early years it could be difficult to get a meeting with many TDs, but as time went on this got easier. As well as her own work for the Coalition she remembered strong lobbying by the Irish Family Planning Association and Amnesty International Ireland.

As the weeks went on the signatures of candidates were gathered by each of the three core organisations, and by polling day 48 TDs elected or re-elected had made that commitment.

As it turned out, the election was quite a disaster for Fine Gael, with the party reduced from 76 seats to 50. It would take months of tortuous negotiations to stitch a confidence-and-supply arrange-ment together with Fianna Fáil and agreements with independent deputies needed to make up the numbers. Katherine Zappone, the former CEO of NWCI, had agreed to support Fine Gael in Government, but insisted she would not sign up to a Programme for Government that did not address a referendum on the Eighth. However a number of independent TDs whom Fine Gael wanted to enlist for their support were standing firm on their objections to any proposed changes. As ever on the abortion issue, it was complicated.

The 2016 election was the first time there were gender quotas for female candidates – with political parties having to implement a 30 per cent gender quota for candidates or have their State funding cut by half. It was a breakthrough election for women, with more than 22 per cent of TDs in the 32nd Dáil being female, compared to the 15 per cent elected in 2011. Orla believes this significant increase did make a difference to how the abortion issue was handled in the Oireachtas, certainly in terms of the subsequent cooperation between parties and between women within parties that would occur. In the previous Dáil there had been a series of bills from left-wing TDs, but now amongst the new female TDs were more openly pro-choice deputies.

Previous to this there were a handful of independent deputies and smaller political parties that had kept raising the issue, some-times bringing forward legislation. But for the vast majority of our elected representatives this was a subject to be avoided, either because they were strongly anti-abortion or because they believed it would not play well with constituents to be seen to be supporting a change in the law to make it more available.

But times were changing and shortly after the election the Coali-tion held a briefing in Buswells Hotel for the deputies and senators from all parties and independents who had publicly pledged to support Repeal, and they agreed to make it a key point on their agenda. These connections and the links between the politicians and the Coalition would prove in time to be key as the communication between both sides opened up.

All the while she was doing the lobbying, Ailbhe always stressed to politicians the growing strength of the Coalition – from that initial membership of 12 to eventually over 120 groups:

"Our strategy certainly was to build to a big number of organisations, because there is power in the numbers. I remember going in and telling TDs there were 50 organisations, and you could see they were impressed with that, and then that it had grown to 70. To be sure some of those organisations were small; nonetheless they could see the Coalition just kept growing."

As well as ARC and NWCI and all of the pro-choice groups, there were human rights organisations, centre-left and radical-left parties, trade unions and NGOs. Ailbhe explained:

"We knew our weaknesses and our strengths and we had laid out and followed an effective strategic path during those years, while also taking the measure of the opposition. Educating the politicians was urgently necessary. We had to inform them about abortion as well as work on the allaying of political fears. There could be no referendum unless the Government agreed to call one and no government was likely to do so unless it was satisfied there was enough support for it in government parties and the Oireachtas more broadly, as well as a reasonable chance of getting a favourable result. It was a huge challenge to break through the reticence of the vast majority of elected representatives to convince them that a referendum was both necessary and winnable. So we had to struggle and strategise and campaign every step of the way."

4

Learning to Talk about Abortion

~~~~~~~~~~~~~~~~~~~~~~~~~~~~~~~~~

The abortion debate is never an easy one, regardless of the country in which it is being conducted. But over the decades Ireland appeared to carve out quite the niche in terms of the bitterness and division created. Practically everyone knew someone who had 'travelled', but the topic would not usually have been seen as everyday conversation anywhere. The enmity often created by the subject meant it seemed to fall almost entirely off the conversation landscape among ordinary Irish people. That was unless it was raised in the media or there was a case such as that of Savita Halappanavar.

To ask the average Irish person, outside of campaigners and activists, to give their take on the abortion issue over decades would likely have resulted in a shoulder shrug and an eye roll. This was a debate characterised in people's minds by shouting, bitterness, recalcitrance, and every few years a tragedy. After decades where it was the subject of a war of words and legal battles and votes, there was an instinctive urge by individuals to stay away from it as a topic, but then if pushed on an opinion to be not quite sure how to vocalise it.

In autumn 2015 Ailbhe approached Adam May, director of the advertising and design agency Language, whom she had worked with before, on behalf of the Coalition to Repeal the Eighth Amendment. She asked him to begin work on an abortion referendum campaign. The research plan developed during 2016, and the Coalition invited the Irish Council for Civil Liberties, NWCI, Amnesty International Ireland, ARC, the Irish Family Planning Association and the Union of Students in Ireland to become partners in the research. Working with researcher Karen Hand, the first focus group was conducted in November 2016.

There were six groups – two in Dublin; two in Mullingar, Co. Westmeath; and the final two in Tralee, Co. Kerry. Adam said it was important to get a real sense of how people were feeling outside of Dublin – 'the pro-choice bubble'. In polling terms he explained that Leinster is usually split into Dublin and 'the rest of Leinster' because it can be considerably more conservative than the capital. One of the reasons they chose Mullingar was its proximity to Roscommon, which was the only county to vote No in the marriage equality referendum. They felt Tralee would give an urban perspective, but also rural. There was one session per group, but in focus group terms it was a long and detailed session, lasting over two hours.

As Adam explained, there is a divergence of views amongst the general public on just about every issue, and many reasons why people might be 'for' or 'against' something. People will have their reasons and it is the job of the campaign to find out what those are.

The first task was to find out what differentiated the centre ground among Irish people from activists on the Yes and No sides.

When it came to abortion it was clear from opinion polls there was a large majority of Irish people who would only support the provision of abortion in certain, restricted circumstances. They were troubled by the status quo, but also wary of change. They sought solutions but were unable to identify what those might be. Any campaign wishing to be successful needed to get a sense of specific tactics and how they would play out with the Irish public.

One of the most important things the research confirmed initially was that people simply did not speak about abortion, and as a result they didn't have the language with which to talk about it. They also didn't have the facts. Adam recalled:

> "It was really interesting what the polarisation of the debate over decades had resulted in. The ugliness of the debate had actually driven it to that, and created a level of ignorance and an inability to grasp the issue for the majority of people. They recoiled from the aggressiveness. They were afraid to bring it up as a subject because you didn't know where someone else was coming from on it and you were scared of what reaction you might get."

People were also saying a lot of complex and conditional things about abortion; how there should be limits and that the idea of having to travel to England was a kind of check on it, because it allowed people to take the time and think about it.

> "There are emotional trade-offs no matter what you think is right or wrong – allowing abortion or restricting it. Then there was an Irish media seen as basically stoking the fire and looking for a scrap between the sides. Going into the research we had the idea there was some sort of soft continuum between the pro-choice and the pro-life lobbies. In fact, what we learned was that the public see themselves as outside the debate. They basically see it as a colosseum where you've got two gladiators locked in combat and they didn't feel that it belonged to them, yet they knew they were impacted by it."

But this very valuable early research showed that, very similar to the marriage equality referendum, people wanted the outcome to be caring and humane; they wanted it to represent the kind of Ireland that they really felt existed. The research group discussion was focused on the concerns of those people, why they would support change and who they would listen to when it came to information on abortion.

The undecided are often spoken about in disparaging terms or described as the 'muddled middle', according to Adam, adding that you cannot begin to communicate with people if you don't respect them. He saw the challenge as communicating with that middle ground. This centre ground, the research found, was thoughtful and caring and realistic about the need for change, but they felt emotionally torn on the issue. They wanted gradual change, not 'mainstreaming'. They wanted there to be a reason for an abortion. They also appreciated honest straight-talking. To be clear, the middle ground were not 'soft' yes voters; they did not support abortion without restrictions.

The research confirmed the clichés about floodgates; people wanted doctors to be involved in the decision and they were not afraid to acknowledge the developing life of the foetus. That acknowledgement was very important to them. Previous abortion campaigns had done everything to avoid acknowledging that. But the research showed that people had no problem acknowledging there is a baby and not to do so was to be seen as being partial with the truth and not recognising reality. It was important to acknowledge two lives, but they were not viewed as being of the same value.

How were the research conclusions received by the client? Ailbhe had assembled the group, made up of ARC, the Irish Council for Civil Liberties, Amnesty International Ireland, the Irish Family Planning Association, NWCI, and the Union of Students in Ireland. When they met with Adam and Karen, Adam noticed there was a sense of "ears pricking up, of realising there is another way, there is something we can do here." At the same time the group, not surprisingly, had reservations about expressing abortion as a need, rather than a right. A key lesson from the research was that people wanted a safe space to listen, think and talk. They wanted a caring outcome for women and families. When the debate turned angry they tended to withdraw.

A clear need for information was revealed among those who wanted to change but found themselves ill-equipped to think about abortion, let alone talk about it. They needed a moral basis for change. They also needed recognition of their own emotional conflict. It was a real revelation, said Adam, that the public had a strong ethical position on this but didn't have both sides of the moral argument so they could weigh it up for themselves:

"This was a really important insight to factor into the campaign. You can't assert rights without having established the moral basis. To do so is just to shout people down. They are wrong if they do not agree with you. The public needed the emotional conflict to be recognised, and this was what we had to establish in order to have people to listen to you, let alone talk to themselves: to be able to establish from the outset that there are negative outcomes with both positions."

Arising from the information they had garnered, the researchers created questions to be used in opinion polling. A key difference to their approach in framing these questions was to word it in such a way that people were being asked to 'enable care'. What the polling allowed them to show was a clear distinction between those who supported the introduction of abortion 'without restriction', and those who supported abortion under the care of a doctor, or restricted by term limits.

In November 2017 the Coalition commissioned a poll on attitudes to abortion. In essence, they created three options within the Yes. There was Yes without restriction or 'on request', Yes with doctor's care, and Yes with term limits.

"Nobody really understood what 12 weeks' gestation meant, or what 24 weeks meant, so in the polling we used the phrase 'with term limits' as a way of creating another parameter that would be a restriction or a controlled provision," explained Adam May. "In the poll we allowed both of those options, and what we found was that firstly the level of support for abortion increases if you look at the 'on request' option, compared to the straight Yes/No options." Suddenly, using this manner of asking, the 'on request' abortion has a much bigger support, and it meant you could see where the conditional supporters were; the overlap between the setting down of term limits and the care of doctors, and the importance of those to people, was also evident.

As a result of the focus group research, the November 2017 poll also contained questions on three issues which had emerged as key problem areas: one was a diagnosis of severe mental disability (of the foetus) in pregnancy, the second was a diagnosis of severe physical disability, and the third a diagnosis of Down syndrome, which is itself a diagnosis of a serious physical or mental disability. Poll responses mirrored exactly the findings from the qualitative research. People saw a diagnosis of severe physical or mental disabilities as being reasonable grounds for making an abortion decision. But if Down syndrome was the reason there was less support.

What could be seen from this was that there was a group who were supporting abortion with restrictions, and a group who were not supporting restrictions, and then there were the straight Nos. As Adam May explained:

"So any perspective that there were soft Yeses who could be brought over to the No side was wrong. And so we developed this idea of that 'concerned centre' as a distinct group. The support for Yes was full of qualifications and reservations. This led us to realise that when you use language of 'no restrictions', which is the familiar language of choice, you give the concerned centre something in common with those who say 'never under any circumstances'. It means they both share what they don't want. But if we can express those restrictions or regulations, if we can talk about it being a private decision, about the need for abortion, about when it is medically necessary, and if we can acknowledge that it's never easy, that it should be regu-lated, and it should be under a doctor's care, then you give them something in common with those who support 'no restriction'. They both support this desire for change. That was absolutely seminal to the campaign messaging strategy. Of course, when you frame it in this way, you can also see the kind of challenges this throws up for people who have been campaigning for choice for decades."

Another part of this qualitative work was to ask people if they knew somebody who had had an abortion. One in three did so. Without any doubt at all there was a correlation between the support for 'no restrictions', and people who knew somebody who had had an abortion. The question was, how to communicate that? How to extend the circle of impact away from the individual woman to everyone who knows and loves her?

Among the many aspects of voter sentiment the research revealed was that the most trusted people in relation to abortion were medical professionals with relevant clinical experience of the welfare of women and babies.

The research showed that medical professionals are crucial for those who are concerned, but not for those who have a clear 'Yes' position, and not for those who have an absolute 'No' position. One of the poll questions asked who should be the person who is best placed to protect babies in the womb, because one of the strongest arguments on the No side was that the Constitution is the only legal protection that the 'unborn' have. Interestingly, people, without any real reservations, said the pregnant woman is the right person.

What the research findings pointed to was that pitching the campaign as 'pro-choice' would alienate a huge segment of supporters because this would deny the motivation of a majority of those who actually supported change but did not identify them-selves as pro-choice.

The research also found that politicians would 'sit on the fence', which, if anything, might provoke a protest vote. It also showed that the Catholic Church was broadly disregarded by people as out of touch and morally precarious, although probably unsurprisingly Catholic beliefs still played a role in people's moral compass.

The research brought sharply into focus the conclusion that after decades of polarisation it was vital to listen to and talk calmly with people who were undecided, and trust them to come to their own conclusions. Empathy was key. People did care. They sought solutions. They simply were not sure what those solutions might be and how they might work.

This brought its own challenges. Traditionally, the fight for abortion rights had been just that: a fight. Each side setting down either its demand to allow abortion, or to continue to ban it. This referendum was a once-in-a-generation chance to change the law and it was almost impossible for some to imagine that a softer, gentler, reasoned approach was the best way forward.

Aware of their common ground, but also their differences, a two-day meeting of organisations had been arranged in Wicklow for October 2016. Looking back, Gráinne, Ailbhe and Orla described it as a 'milestone'. Despite any differences they had there was far more common ground between them, and they reached agreement there on a number of key issues. The meeting was organised by the Centre for Reproductive Rights, the global legal advocacy organisation dedicated to reproductive rights. In advance each group was sent a survey to sound out opinions on different topics. These were filled in by NWCI, ARC, the Coalition, Amnesty and the Irish Family Planning Association.

There were discussions about abortion on demand and its availability in other countries. There was particular interest in Spain, which adopted legislation in 2010 allowing abortion on demand up to fourteen weeks, and up to twenty-two weeks under certain conditions, including foetal deformities or if the mother's health is at risk. At that meeting it was realised that the various demands of different groups needed to be prioritised. The results of the survey were used as a guide.

Decriminalisation of abortion was clearly important, but so too was abortion access on request. Looking at both of these issues, the participants discussed how many people were affected in each instance: clearly abortion on request would make a much bigger difference to a larger number of women. Protecting women's right to access abortion care in the event of a risk to their health was seen as a very high priority, and not just a serious health risk, as was also the case for fatal foetal abnormality. But there was general concern that what would end up being proposed in a referendum would be a very restrictive regime based only on access to abortion in cases of rape and for fatal foetal abnormality.

The different groups participating in that meeting knew that demands had to be prioritised. In the end they agreed they could ultimately 'live with' abortion access up to fourteen weeks, although no one intended saying this publicly at that point. This was a pragmatic recognition that at some point proposed legislation would spell out a number of weeks and they would need to have decided in advance where they all stood on this contentious aspect. There was also the reality that the vast majority of women who were having abortions were doing so early. For instance, in 2015 in England and Wales 81 per cent of abortions were carried out at between three and nine weeks' gestation.

Inherent in all of this was an acceptance that different groups would be saying different things in public, with their own priorities. However they agreed that no one would 'throw the other under a bus' in forthcoming debates and discussions, and the inevitable efforts by the media to cause division.

5

The Citizens' Assembly: Gasps of Surprise and Delight

~~~~~~

The proposal that the abortion question be sent to an assembly for consideration by a group of citizens, and then to have their recommendations sent on to Government, was greeted with almost universal dismay by those who had been fighting for so long for change. The Coalition to Repeal the Eighth Amendment described it as yet another "delaying tactic" by then Taoiseach Enda Kenny.

Orla and NWCI were very sceptical because she had believed an actual date for a referendum was close but that this was a way for Fine Gael and Fianna Fáil to potentially wriggle out of dealing with the issue.

Gráinne and ARC felt beyond frustrated with the "political manoeuvring" which they believed was a mechanism for Fine Gael to distance themselves from the inevitable conclusion that there needed to be a referendum on the Eighth Amendment.

An earlier Convention on the Constitution, established in 2012, had recommended a referendum on same-sex marriage. In May 2016, in response to growing pressure to address the issue of abortion, the new minority Government committed to establishing a Citizens' Assembly to be charged with making recommendations on the Eighth Amendment. It differed in one important respect from the Convention on the Constitution in that its membership was composed entirely of 'randomly selected' citizens, whereas the earlier body had included politicians as one-third of its membership.

The Citizens' Assembly would be chaired by former Supreme Court Judge Mary Laffoy and while abortion had top billing, other, less high-profile, issues to be considered were climate change and referendum procedures. Five of the Assembly's meetings, from January to April 2017, focused exclusively on abortion, over 90 hours in total. This was to be an exercise in non-parliamentary deliberative democracy. But given all that had gone on previously with this guaranteed-to-incite-anger issue, it was virtually impossible to imagine how it was going to work out.

The logic seemed to be that this particular exercise in democracy would, at its conclusion, lead to a referendum on the Eighth Amendment. The Assembly led to "robust discussion" within the Coalition. According to Ailbhe, many member organisations viewed the Assembly as a cynical move. The instinct was to not engage with it at all, while others felt that had to be done:

"But for myself, and the leadership of the Coalition, there was no question but that we had to engage with this particular exercise. The Constitutional Convention had worked well for marriage equality. I felt this was absolutely crucial. It was going to be livestreamed; it was going to be very public. It was a way for us to push our message out and raise public awareness. It was about building and recruiting and we worked hard to bring our members with us. We held a press conference with a cross-section of members to emphasise the breadth of concerns but also indicating we would be supporting the work of the Assembly."

There would be controversy over the selection of the 99 participant citizens, a task which had been awarded to the polling company Red C by the Department of the Taoiseach during the summer of 2016. It was instructed to find a group of people representative of the population in age, gender, class and urban/rural residence in favour of change, against it and undecided. One of the most vocal critics of the Assembly was independent Tipperary TD Mattie McGrath, a high-profile anti-abortion politician who described the recruitment process as a "debacle", saying eleven counties, including his own, had been excluded from the Assembly. He questioned how that could be fair or democratic by any measure.

The Assembly had its first meeting in Dublin Castle on 15 October 2016, where the Taoiseach, Enda Kenny, thanked the members for participating and said that in doing so they were putting their heads above the parapet. The issue of abortion had divided our nation in the past:

"You [the members] have been asked to perform a unique civic duty, which is above and beyond what you have ever done before. It will require not only a substantial time commitment, but dedication to the process. I would ask that everybody recognise the complexity and the challenge of the task and give the citizens the respect, freedom and space to do their work."

For her part that day, Ms Justice Laffoy said it was critical to the Assembly's success and integrity that, "members can freely and confidently make contributions and express their views without fear of harassment or criticism".

After the pomp of Dublin Castle the Assembly settled down to monthly meetings at a hotel in Malahide, and each weekend they listened to people on both sides of the abortion debate, including experts and those sharing their personal experiences. The Assembly secretariat was very ably led by senior civil servant Sharon Finegan. On that first Saturday morning, and subsequently, anti-abortion protesters stood at the gate to the hotel holding up posters with graphic photographs of foetuses.

Inside the hotel, though, there was an absence of this sort of drama. From the beginning it was clear that these meetings would be a rare thing in Ireland – a public discussion on abortion which did not descend into a shouting match.

The proceedings would garner considerable interest among the public and after the Assembly invited submissions from the public it received a mountain of testimony over a two-month period at the end of 2016. These were from both sides of the debate, with well over 13,000 submissions received, over 8,000 of which were online and almost 5,000 by post. Anonymous submissions were not accepted, but in the case of personal stories and what was described as "sensitive submissions" all personal data could be removed from the website if requested.

Over the five weekends the citizens heard from 40 experts in medicine, law and ethics. They discussed matters relating to crisis pregnancy, termination of pregnancy, suicide in pregnancy, foetal abnormalities, the regimes that exist abroad, sex education, ethics, morals, freedom of choice, rape, and how the medical profession is regulated.

Ailbhe remembered those Saturdays in Malahide and the process of watching the citizens settle into their role, gradually feeling more at ease and more knowledgeable and asking more questions:

"In the first few sessions the citizen members were not jumping up and down to ask questions and make points. They had their discussion groups and the facilitator for each table would report back and this would all be noted, then everybody would sit down again and the next experts would be brought in, and the discussion group would happen again. And the facilitator would report back. But around weekend number three individual table members were getting up and saying 'this is the view of our table.' Then somebody else at the table would say 'oh now hold on a minute, there was another view here.' So there was much more determined, obvious discussion and debate. They felt more at ease. They were clearly becoming bolder, more informed and confident.

I had realised that first weekend that we were not allowed to consort in any way with the members after I had inadvertently joined a particular coffee queue and it was very nicely pointed out to me that this was for Assembly members only and observers' coffee was somewhere else. So the next week I watched everything and by the third weekend, as soon as the break came, I rushed into the loo because that's where I would hear the women chatting about it."

During the second weekend that they had gathered to consider the Eighth Amendment, ten of the fourteen tables answered "no" to the question "Should the right to life of the unborn child continue to be constitutionally protected in the same way as now?" It was a key moment.

Another was the session during which the Assembly members heard from six women directly affected by the Eighth, some of whose stories went back decades. The Assembly secretariat organised for these women to have their stories recorded in advance and on the day in question the audio was played as the citizens listened intently.

From the wide range of groups that made submissions to the Assembly the members were asked who they wished to present to them in person. The final decision was left to Ms Justice Laffoy, who said balance needed to be assured. In all seventeen groups presented, each given ten minutes.

NWCI was chosen, as was the Coalition to Repeal the Eighth Amendment, although ARC was disappointed not to be included as by that stage it was one of the largest organisations working exclusively on abortion access. The other groups who presented were

Doctors for Life Ireland, Doctors for Choice, the Union of Students in Ireland, Youth Defence, Women Hurt, Parents for Choice, Every Life Counts, the Irish Family Planning Association, Family & Life, the Pro Life Campaign, Amnesty International Ireland, the Iona Institute, the Irish Catholic Bishops' Conference, Atheist Ireland, and the General Synod of the Church of Ireland.

ARC did dedicate a lot of time and resources to preparing a comprehensive submission. The group was particularly concerned that an attempt would be made to replace the Eighth Amendment with another restrictive amendment allowing only very limited access in situations that did not apply to the vast majority of women accessing abortion. Under the heading 'Why We Need Free, Safe, Legal Abortion Access', the ARC submission stated that it believed that barrier-free access to abortion constituted best practice in healthcare. As a society, it said, we rarely speak about abortion as a positive choice. ARC strongly believed that for women to have meaningful control over their bodies "they must have access to safe, affordable abortion care, as and when they need or want it. Anything less than this constitutes a restriction on the personal liberty and bodily autonomy of women." The group also said that it opposed gestational limits for abortion "because we do not believe there should ever be a time limit on accessing healthcare". "There is no right or wrong time to have an abortion, just as no one reason for accessing abortion services outweighs the other."

Restrictions are all too frequently premised on public perceptions of 'good' and 'bad' abortions, said the submission. There has been much discussion in Ireland about allowing access to abortion in cases of rape and incest. These situations are horrific, and women should undoubtedly be able to terminate pregnancies resulting from grievous assaults. But if abortion was only available under these circumstances how could women access abortion services without them having to 'prove' their trauma in an invasive way? "In your discussion we would ask the Citizens' Assembly to seriously consider why abortion is more acceptable when women have suffered", ARC asked.

It pointed out that a significant number of international institutions and monitoring bodies had criticised Irish abortion law.

"Ireland is one of the only countries in Europe to maintain such restrictive abortion practices."

Most importantly, the ARC submission included the stories of 60 people who had been affected by the Eighth Amendment. The group felt that women's stories and narratives were central to the process and had put out a call on social media for people to submit their story for inclusion. It was originally intended to name the authors but there was concern that women who has accessed abortion illegally might face consequences if they publicly admitted to breaking the law.

Ultimately, ARC held the personal details of the authors and submitted their stories anonymously:

"Some of these stories are upsetting. They are varied, but they are united in one thing: they all express the simple truth that the 8th Amendment is not fit for purpose. The 8th Amendment did not stop them from having an abortion. It did however make them feel isolated and alone, exiled from Ireland. Many talk of shame and stigma and most chose to be anonymous."

When it came to the turn of the Coalition to present, Ailbhe gave a resume of its written submission, telling the citizens the issue they had been asked to consider was much more than a constitutional issue: it was a medical issue, a human rights issue, an equality issue, a social class issue and a feminist issue.

The Eighth Amendment, she said, was a profound source of discrimination and inequality for the many women in Ireland for whom travel was not an option. "The right to travel does not guarantee equal access to treatment as many women who need an abortion are unable to travel for a variety of reasons, while others are specifically prevented from doing so by the State. The abortion ban hits marginalised and vulnerable women the hardest", she explained, outlining the hardships for women on low incomes, asylum-seekers and undocumented women, women with disabilities, and victims of domestic violence.

Addressing the issue of fatal foetal abnormality, she said those women and couples were severely impacted by the Eighth

Amendment: "Denying people options in such very sad circumstances cannot be regarded as support."

Under the heading of 'Autonomy and Choice', Ailbhe told the members that reproductive autonomy is a cornerstone of women's struggle to achieve independence and equality worldwide:

"We must in our laws acknowledge the totality and complexity of women's lives including their health and well-being, their relationships and family life, their responsibilities and social circumstances, their working lives and their financial situation, their ability to cope, and – not least – their wishes and plans, hopes and dreams. It is not enough to provide treatment only in medical emergencies and only then where there's a 'real and substantial risk' to a woman's life as opposed to her health. This very narrow value we ascribe to women's lives is a damning indictment of our laws and not at all reflective of the caring society we are."

Speaking for the Coalition, Ailbhe said the members were calling for the Eighth Amendment to be repealed in its entirety from the Constitution with no further amendment proposed to replace it. Abortion, including medical abortion – the abortion pill – should be decriminalised and current abortion laws – the Protection of Life During Pregnancy Act 2013 and the Abortion Information Act 1995 – should be repealed. New regulatory frameworks, with women's autonomy as a core principle, should be put in place to ensure women's equal and unimpeded access to the highest attainable standards of reproductive healthcare, including abortion.

When Orla spoke on behalf of NWCI she highlighted how the failure to provide abortion services in Ireland created considerable psychological, physical and emotional hardship for those who were either forced to travel outside the country for abortion or purchase medication illegally, or forced to continue with an unwanted pregnancy and to parent because of restrictions imposed on them.

The Eighth Amendment, she said, was reflective of Irish society at the time of its enactment to the Constitution in 1983: an Ireland in which women were incarcerated in workhouses for bearing children out of wedlock or leaving abusive husbands; in which contraceptives could only be dispensed by a pharmacist on the presentation of a valid medical prescription from a practising doctor; and in which divorce and homosexuality were illegal, but marital rape was not. It reflected a society which didn't trust women to make choices about their own lives.

"Women in Ireland make the decision to have an abortion for a variety and combination of reasons," she said. Women's lived experiences are multi-faceted, inherently personal and they change over the course of their lifetime. All of our lives are complex. As Orla elaborated:

> "Our decisions are based on a whole variety of circumstances, our backgrounds, our future aspirations for ourselves and the people we love around us. The decision to parent is one of the most significant decisions a woman will make. It will affect everything about her future thereafter."

In the context of fear of criminal prosecution, medical professionals were effectively prevented from exercising clinical discretion in their patients' best interests and applying best clinical practice by intervening when a health risk presents. A HSE report into the tragic death of Savita Halappanavar while in receipt of maternity care in University Hospital Galway in 2012, said Orla, found that the uncertainty created by Ireland's abortion laws was a "material contributory factor" in her death.

Orla said that in almost every other European country women were legally allowed to access abortion in early pregnancy when they request it, and in these circumstances, what is considered to be 'early pregnancy' can vary between 10 and 24 weeks. In the countries that do not explicitly provide for early access to abortion at a women's request (Finland, Iceland and the United Kingdom), they specify this access can be granted with the opinion of two medical professionals:

"In practice, the laws in these countries are interpreted and applied in a manner that means that when a woman believes that ending a pregnancy is the best decision for her, with reference to her personal, social and economic circumstances, she is usually able to legally access services within the specified time-limits. Best practice, however, would prescribe legal clarity."

All of the European, and other, countries that allow abortion on request also permit medical professionals to perform abortions later in pregnancy within the context of certain specified exceptional circumstances – these include risks to the women's health or life and situations of serious or fatal foetal impairment.

Orla told the Assembly that:

"... providing for early medical abortion on request in Ireland would be a means of responding to the evident needs of women, removing the stigma, shame and other burdens of the current system and would remove cumbersome and unwieldy criminal sanctions against women and medical professionals. It would provide for access to abortion to women in particularly vulnerable positions in a manner that protects their dignity, privacy and bodily autonomy. Where a wanted pregnancy becomes a crisis pregnancy by becoming a risk to her health, or due to a diagnosis of fatal foetal anomaly, provisions should be made for later-term terminations."

Developing the submission was an intense process for NWCI, said Orla. It was decided it would not be enough to simply recommend repeal but there also needed to be a discussion about what would come afterwards. There was major concern in NWCI that rape would be singled out as a ground for an abortion and that a woman would be forced to disclose a rape in order to access what should be a public health service.

"This conversation led to a decision by the board and staff that we needed to strongly recommend that a grounds approach to

> abortion will not work for women, and there must be a period where no reason was required to access abortion and that we needed to publicly state early pregnancy based on best international evidence and on what could be possibly achieved in Ireland."

So this was the first time NWCI advocated a period of 'on request' abortion in early pregnancy.

The Citizens' Assembly gave an opportunity for both sides of the abortion debate to take the measure of each other and to see what, if any, new arguments or approaches were being taken. As far as Gráinne was concerned, the performance of the No side in their Assembly presentations "was designed to shock; it was very emotive, very dramatic and very gruesome. They really didn't meet the conversation where it was at in Ireland." She felt it was a mistake for two of those groups chosen to present – Youth Defence and Women Hurt – to ask representatives from the United States to speak on their behalf.

Rebecca Kiessling, a US attorney who describes herself as a "pro-life speaker conceived in rape", spoke for Youth Defence and said abortion was loved by "sex traffickers and child molesters. It destroys the evidence. It protects and enables them so that they can continue." American Dr Anthony Levatino, who performed 1,200 abortions in the 1980s, spoke on behalf of Women Hurt, an Irish anti-abortion group for women who regret having abortions. Giving graphic details, he said he had performed second-trimester abortions where he removed arms and legs from aborted foetuses.

"Oh it was so provocative and untrue and so grotesque," remembered Gráinne:

> "We had taken such pains to bring integrity, evidence and the voices of regular women into our work and then they rocked up with these American presenters who were quite outrageous. I felt sorry for the members of the Assembly listening to it. The presenters clearly thought those methods were very effective. The anti-choice movement has been very successful in

the States using those tactics. So it was an attempt to adopt a winning format but while it certainly had a very strong impact on the room, it didn't work; they underestimated the depth of the debate and discussion in the Assembly, but at the time it was very nerve-racking wondering how they had been received."

Orla too found the approach strange. But she also remembered how the other side had concentrated on the issue of abortion following a diagnosis of disability:

"It became very clear the issue of disability was key to them. I suppose that was good for us in terms of knowing – although we probably knew already – that they were going to raise those types of arguments in the referendum campaign and try to use them against us."

The final weekend of the Assembly arrived. On the Saturday morning the citizens sat down knowing they were reaching the end of the road on their exhaustive consideration of the Eighth Amendment. Ms Justice Laffoy told them they had gained an "almost uniquely comprehensive understanding" of the issues relating to abortion in Ireland. Observing the group in all their hours of deliberation, it was remarkable there never appeared to be anything other than full concentration and engagement. The gatherings had been almost exclusively non-combative but that day there were some vexed words between them, as they discussed what exactly they would be voting on, and the briefings they had received on specific legal issues. It was clear they were taking it very seriously.

In the first ballot, members of the Assembly voted overwhelmingly to recommend that the Eighth Amendment should not be retained in its current form.

In the second, 56 per cent voted that it should be amended or replaced and in the subsequent vote 57 per cent recommended that it be replaced with a constitutional provision explicitly authorising the Oireachtas to make laws to address termination of pregnancy, any rights of the unborn, and any rights of the pregnant woman.

In other words, it would be a matter for the Oireachtas to decide how to legislate on these issues.

This result was a shock to many who believed it was potentially disastrous that a vote had been taken not to simply repeal.

"It was nerve-racking", said Ailbhe. "We didn't quite take the measure of it to start with, where they seemed to be saying they wanted to rephrase the Eighth Amendment. We felt worried, very concerned and disappointed at that."

For ARC, this appeared to open the door to the Government ultimately putting forward a more restrictive amendment to replace the Eighth. An abortion referendum was seen as a once-in-a-generation opportunity. Gráinne explained:

> "We worried that there could be divisions over a referendum to replace [the Eighth Amendment]. Ultimately, unless the referendum resolved the issue of twelve women a day travelling to the UK, we wouldn't be able to support it."

The cross words had arisen when some citizens said they had voted for reform of the Eighth Amendment on the basis that Ms Justice Laffoy had advised that repeal might lead to legal uncertainty over the issue of abortion. She ruled out a re-run of the second ballot of the day. The legal consequences of repeal could not be established with certainty, she stressed.

On the Sunday the citizens appeared to have done what the chairperson had urged to "regain collegiality", as they faced into the next task of voting on eight scenarios in which the Oireachtas could legislate for abortion, and also the time limits for such abortions. The final paper presented 40 options to the citizens. There was a buzz of anticipation in the room of what was to come, and what would be decided in the series of upcoming votes. By the end of their deliberations the options on offer on the ballot paper had risen to 65. The citizens approved a proposal to include socioeconomic circumstances as a reason for abortion, considered a very radical proposal, and the final option was changed from 'abortion on request' to 'no restriction as to reason'. That last session ran over by two hours because of the complexity of the ballot.

There were gasps of surprise as some of the multi-option ballot results were revealed, especially from those who had believed the citizens would simply opt for action on rape, incest and fatal foetal abnormalities. But once the result of those votes were in it was abundantly clear, and a shock to almost all present, just how liberal the views of the citizens were on abortion.

The citizens had shown their considerable nous in subsequent votes where they made recommendations to the Oireachtas about what should be included in the legislation – for what reasons, if any, abortion should be lawful in Ireland, as well as any gestational limits that should apply. A majority of the 92 members in attendance voted to allow for abortion in all 13 circumstances considered by the Assembly. An incredible number of them, just under two-thirds, voted that termination of pregnancy without restriction should be made law. Of those, 48 per cent recommended abortion without restriction up to 12 weeks, 44 per cent up to 22 weeks, and 8 per cent with no time restriction.

On top of that, a majority of citizens recommended legalising abortion – with results of 90 per cent and over in each case – where there was a real and substantive risk to the life of the woman, similarly to the life of the woman by suicide, to the physical health of the woman, to the health of the woman and to her mental health. None of the votes when counted went below 72 per cent support, which was the result for socioeconomic reasons, and that reason had been included at the request of members. It rose to 80 per cent for a significant foetal abnormality that is not likely to result in death before or shortly after birth, and 89 per cent for an abnormality likely to result in death before or shortly after birth. Support for abortion where there was a risk to the physical health of the woman, risk to the mental health and risk to health were all just under 80 per cent.

In an additional question, almost three-quarters had agreed that a distinction should be drawn between the physical and mental health of the woman.

The results were more liberal than most would ever have imagined likely. The Citizens' Assembly approved the availability of abortion, in all thirteen circumstances they considered, by wide margins. As Ailbhe remembered:

"We'd been worried, of course, but when the votes started coming in on the individual issues we very quickly realised we were in a landslide situation. It was clear that this Citizens' Assembly, which had started off neutral at best, had decided in their minds that they wanted very liberal abortion legislation, including for socioeconomic reasons. They wanted abortion to be available for up to the first fourteen weeks to protect women's health, without any qualification. They had listened carefully and did what they thought would respond to women's needs. We were absolutely delighted and vindicated because we had all put a lot of time and effort in our different organisations into working with our members and in making presentations, position papers and so on."

The Coalition called a press conference, including NWCI, Amnesty and the Irish Family Planning Association. Orla recalls it as being filled with emotion and also strength: "I remember saying that the citizens of Ireland had put women's lives at the centre of their decisions and now it was up to the Government to do the same. It was a moment that we knew the Government couldn't walk away from."

The Assembly was remarkable for a number of reasons but the chief one being, as Ms Justice Laffoy pointed out, that the members had listened with respect to the voices and opinions of others on the issue of the Eighth Amendment.

Ms Justice Laffoy said there was now a "clear map" for politicians. Taoiseach Enda Kenny, when asked about repeal of the Eighth Amendment, used to be fond of responding, "and what would you replace it with?" Now he had a definitive answer, provided by the citizens. Unsurprisingly, there had not been many moments of levity at these Assembly weekend gatherings. However on that final Sunday there was one. A citizen member asked that TDs and senators on the Oireachtas Committee, which would soon be dealing with the Assembly's recommendations, read all the documentation and transcripts to ensure they ended up as well-informed as the members. "Test them, we don't trust them", he said to the wry laughter of his fellow citizens.

The Assembly, in the words of UCD Professor of Politics David Farrell, had proved invaluable in acquainting the political classes with the fact that the Irish public had become much more liberal in recent decades.

Ailbhe remembered going back into the Dáil after that shock result and how the atmosphere in relation to abortion had "just completely shifted". "Not everybody was overjoyed but they all knew a political reality when they saw it written down in front of them."

6

Trying to Persuade the Politicians

~~~~~~

The fifth anniversary of the death of Savita Halappanavar in a Galway hospital was marked on 28 October 2017. A lesser observed anniversary in Ireland was the 50th anniversary of the Abortion Act, legalising pregnancy terminations in the UK, which occurred just one day before, on 27 October. If Savita's death brought a new impetus to doing something about abortion in Ireland, then the introduction of that UK legislation had meant that for decades Irish abortions were taking place in their hundreds of thousands, but just not on the island of Ireland. It was this that had allowed Irish politicians to turn away from the problem for decades.

But 2017 was the year that abortion was brought front and centre in the Oireachtas. A special committee of TDs and senators was established specifically to consider the report of the Citizens' Assembly. Those Assembly votes had certainly conditioned, not just the politicians, but also the public. There was a weight of expectation now on the political class. The Committee was required to report conclusions and recommendations to the Dáil and Seanad within three months of their first public meeting. But still the doubts lingered: Would they try to rerun the Citizens' Assembly? How different would the political approach be from that body's work? How much might be going on behind the scenes to yet again pitch a referendum into the future?

In June the United Nations Human Rights Committee had ruled for the second time that Ireland's abortion laws violated women's human rights. That ruling had come after an Irish woman, Siobhán Whelan, was denied access to abortion services in Ireland following a diagnosis in 2010 of a fatal foetal impairment. The Committee said that Ireland must provide Ms Whelan with reparations for the harm she suffered and reform its laws to ensure other women did not continue to face similar violations. The previous year the Government had agreed to pay another Irish woman, Amanda Mellet, €30,000 compensation after the UN body found her rights had been violated. Both cases were represented by the Centre for Reproductive Rights. The international pressure kept intensifying.

That June also saw the election of Leo Varadkar as leader of Fine Gael and subsequently Taoiseach. He would say that his view on abortion had "evolved", but seven years earlier, in May 2010, he said in an interview with the *Sunday Independent Life Magazine* that allowing rape victims to terminate their pregnancies could lead to "abortion on demand".

Described at that time as a "conservative TD and medical doctor", Leo Varadkar said he would "not be in favour of abortion" and, although not religious, he would "accept a lot of Catholic social thinking".

He did add that "a grey area is if there's a genuine threat or risk to the life of the mother." But not for victims of rape: "I wouldn't be in favour of it in that case, and, you know, first of all, it isn't the child's fault that they're the child of rape." He was also against abortion in cases of disability.

Despite the thousands of Irish women travelling for abortion each year he did not see a double standard, expressing himself rather bluntly on that issue:

> "People travel overseas to do things overseas that aren't legal in Ireland all the time. You know, are we going to stop people going to Las Vegas? Are we going to stop people going to Amsterdam? There are things that are illegal in Ireland and we don't prevent people from travelling overseas to avail of them."

He would speak on the issue on a number of occasions in the Dáil in different debates. On 9 September 2017, just months after taking office, he said he regarded marriage equality and abortion as very different issues:

> "As a doctor, I would perform pregnancy scans, and while I don't accept the view that the unborn child – the foetus, if you prefer that term – should have equal rights to an adult woman, to the mother, I don't share this view that the baby in the womb – the foetus, whatever term you want to use – should have no rights at all. And there are people who take the view that human rights only begin after you're born and that a child in the womb with a beating heart, the ability to hear, the ability to feel pain, should have no rights whatsoever. I don't agree with that."

But while Leo Varadkar and others continued to grapple with their thoughts and feelings on abortion, the change in Irish society's traditional manner of dealing with the issue continued to be felt. *Irish Times* columnist Róisín Ingle and comedian and writer Tara Flynn had been involved in a conversation around a table with some other women one night. It was in the weeks after the marriage equality referendum and they were discussing how Repeal had to be next on the agenda. Tara took the then unusual step of revealing that she had had an abortion and three others around the table said they had too. She said the feeling of solidarity and relief was incredible. One of the other three was Róisín Ingle. Considered to always be very open about her personal and family life, she would write in the newspaper one Saturday in September 2015 about the secret that she had been keeping for 15 years: the abortion she had had in her late 20s.

"Like tens of thousands of women in Ireland and like hundreds of thousands of women around the world I am glad and relieved and not at all ashamed that I once had an abortion," wrote Róisín. It happened after her five-year marriage had broken up. "I was flailing around in self-loathing mode. Going out too much. Drinking too much. It happened one night."

After taking a pregnancy test she got the "wrong answer". She arranged to meet up with the man she had slept with and they discussed what to do. They were on the same page and agreed to share the cost. A friend travelled to England with her:

> "I booked the clinic. There was no faltering. No indecision. I went to sleep that night relieved and unburdened. It was over. My life could carry on the way it was before. I was going to be more careful in future."

She felt the time was right now to share her story, although she did consult her mother, Ann Ingle, who had concerns about Róisín opening up about the subject and how her readers might react.

Róisín had often been asked if there was something she wouldn't write about and each time what came into her head was the abortion she had had. At that point she felt it was time to hear those personal stories in the abortion conversation:

> "Why am I writing this? Because I want to be a part, however small, of the campaign to change abortion legislation in this country. Because if my daughters come to me and say they are pregnant when they don't want to be, I don't want them to have to get a boat or a train or a plane. I want to mind them at

home where I can put my arms around them and given them a hot-water bottle. I want to support and love and care for them every step of the way. I want to respect their choice. I want them to have a choice. Because most countries in Europe give women that choice. Just not the one in which I live."

As Róisín was preparing for publication of that article, Tara Flynn got a call from Colm O'Gorman, executive director of Amnesty International Ireland, asking would she MC a gig for Amnesty at the Electric Picnic festival. It would focus on Amnesty's global 'She is not a criminal' campaign on reproductive rights, making it specific to Ireland. Tara decided to use this as her opportunity to talk about her own abortion in 2006, where emergency contraception failed and she found herself having to fly to Utrecht in the Netherlands for a termination.

"And so I told my story in a tent in rural County Laois while basslines boomed from nearby stages. People in the tent stood up and spoke of their own journeys", she wrote in a piece in *The Guardian*:

"They cried. I cried. I've barely stopped since. That same week, Róisín's story was published. We got abuse, both vicious and vocal. We were told we were 'too much', that we were scaring people. But we knew that wasn't true. We knew that, if we all just kept talking to each other, people would find out. That the woman sitting next to you on the bus is 'that woman'. That the woman on the telly is. Your daughter is. You could be. I am that woman. Conversations have been had all across the country. Tears shed. Hands held. And those conversations shattered secrets and shame and gave faces to a hidden issue."

Then less than two weeks after becoming Taoiseach, on the day he announced his Cabinet, Leo Varadkar confirmed an abortion referendum would take place sometime in the next year, 2018. But doubts remained about where exactly he stood. That September at the March for Choice in Dublin, there were chants of "My body, my choice" and "Hey, hey Leo, the Eighth Amendment has to go", as well as signs reading, "Get off the fence Leo". Shortly after he assumed office, Canadian Prime Minister Justin Trudeau came to Ireland on an official visit. Orla was invited to the official dinner at Dublin Castle and remembered being in the receiving line at the event. Before she reached Prime Minister Trudeau she knew there would be a few words with the Taoiseach. As she moved along she was thinking what she would say to him about the referendum.

"So when the time came I said, 'this will be one of the most critical times for women in Ireland'. And he said [she laughed wryly as she remembered the exchange], 'Do you think we're going to win?' And I said 'Yes I do', and he said 'Well I really hope you are right.' And I remember thinking then, 'We better win.' It felt like the full pressure was on us to deliver Repeal in the referendum."

As far as Gráinne was concerned there were certain politicians and political parties which were supporters of the cause but ARC did not count Leo Varadkar as one of those. "We had our allies but Leo Varadkar was not going to introduce abortion into Ireland unless he had to."

Then all eyes were on the Oireachtas Committee on the Eighth Amendment. The task of the 21-person committee was to draft the proposed changes to Ireland's abortion laws following recommendations made by the Citizens' Assembly. The legislators had been handed over the responsibility to pass abortion law.

In the run-up to it there was a sense this large and ungainly committee was hugely divided before it ever began its work, with both sides stuck in their trenches. A number were said not to even want to be on the Committee, believing it to be a poisoned chalice which would bring abuse down on their heads and complications with their constituents. It was known there was going to be a referendum the following year but there were ongoing and understandable concerns that what would happen in between times could be rather tortuous, and that the Citizens' Assembly proposals could get tossed around like a political football.

As far as Gráinne and ARC were concerned, the Committee was yet another unnecessary step on the road to a referendum that just seemed constantly out of actual reach:

> "It was a case of 'oh dear God, will it never end?' The Committee was widely seen as an opportunity to water down the very progressive position put forward by the Citizens' Assembly and actually it did in part do that in the end. The months were passing and we were so aware that women continued to travel on a daily basis."

Nor did Ailbhe feel particularly joyful at the prospect of it:

> "We were thinking, oh heavens, this is another year of our lives, another year of four or five thousand women travelling over to Britain. But the more sensible, strategic and rational part of me was thinking this is important: it's about the legislation, it has to go through the hoops. We have to pay close attention and be prepared to provide back-up, information and support – whatever is needed."

Fine Gael senator Catherine Noone was appointed Committee chairperson. Reflecting the prevailing mood, her task was acknowledged as Herculean. Feelings on the issue generally were running high in Leinster House as both sides attempted to claim the higher ground. The Committee was considered to have a majority in favour of liberalising in some shape the State's strict abortion laws. But Senator Noone would have to juggle, for instance, the beliefs of independent senator Rónán Mullen and independent TD Mattie McGrath on one side, both vocally and staunchly anti-abortion, while on the other were pro-choice Solidarity TD Ruth Coppinger, Independents 4 Change TD Clare Daly, and Fine Gael's Kate O'Connell, who had given her take on abortion: "as early as possible and as late as necessary".

Between them Fine Gael and Fianna Fáil did have a majority on the Committee and neither Fine Gael nor Fianna Fáil members were subject to a party whip, allowing them to vote with their conscience. Thus there was no guarantee of an outcome, especially as there were very different views even within each party grouping. The Government's position was unknown. There was an expectation the Committee would recommend legislating for abortion only in certain circumstances, including rape, incest and fatal foetal abnormalities.

The report of the Citizens' Assembly had been published in June. Ms Justice Laffoy and the Assembly secretariat produced an 83-page document and two large volumes of appendices, running to almost 1,000 pages and containing all the complex facts and expert testimony previously absorbed by the citizens.

As time was going on newspaper opinion polls during this period would make clear that Irish voters were in favour of the repeal of the Eighth Amendment. There was definitely a public appetite for a loosening of our strict abortion laws.

Interestingly though, a majority of voters were not in favour of abortion on request, such as the regime that existed in the UK. A further *Irish Times* IPSOS/MRBI opinion poll in June 2017, after the Citizens' Assembly report was delivered, found that many of the Assembly findings, where abortion should be allowed, found favour with the public, including rape and fatal foetal abnormalities. However when asked if they backed abortion being allowed "where a woman believes she would be unable to cope because of her age or circumstances", only 28 per cent approved.

Separately, however, Amnesty International Ireland had conducted three opinion polls on abortion, carried out by the Red C polling company. A poll in November 2017 was based on the ballot wording put to the Citizens' Assembly. It showed that, of those who had an opinion, a majority of people in Ireland – 60 per cent – believed that women should have access to abortion on request, either outright or within specific gestational limits.

The first Amnesty poll in July 2015 showed that 81 per cent of people were in favour of significantly widening the grounds for access to legal abortions in Ireland. The second poll in February 2016 showed an overwhelming 87 per cent of people in favour of expanded access to abortion and that 80 per cent would vote to repeal the Eighth Amendment.

When she appeared before the Oireachtas Committee, Ms Justice Laffoy urged the politicians to look into reports about the widespread use of abortion pills by Irish women – pills usually obtained by post. She was concerned that after the Assembly report had been completed the HSE crisis pregnancy agency put online up-to-date statistics showing the number of women going to the UK and Netherlands for terminations reducing. But there were increasing numbers of women in Ireland making contact with online pill providers. "I think that's a factor you should look at", she said.

As the politicians were settling into their work Leo Varadkar said he did not believe the country was ready for abortion on demand. He promised the next referendum held by the Government would be on the Eighth Amendment but he didn't know what options would be given to voters:

> "I honestly don't know if the public would go as far as what the Citizens' Assembly have recommended. Public opinion polls have indicated that they wouldn't but that may change during the course of the debate and having observed the Citizens' Assembly and how that debate evolved, we have become aware of the availability of abortion pills and how they work. It is actually quite possible that people's views may change as we have the debate."

Indeed abortion pills would play a key role from here on in. When Dr Peter Boylan, chairman of the Institute of Obstetricians and Gynaecologists of Ireland, appeared at the Committee he said the "genie was out of the bottle" when it came to abortion in Ireland because of the availability of these pills. He highlighted the irony of how the medicine, although illegal in Ireland, could now be accessed using semi-State company An Post's AddressPal, which gives a virtual address in the UK and delivers to Ireland.

The master of the Rotunda, Professor Fergal Malone, also spoke of concerns about women using this medication. Women do not know what they are taking, he told the Committee. While the master of the National Maternity Hospital in Holles Street, Dr Rhona Mahony, spoke of the circumstances in which a young person might choose to obtain tablets from a source she did not know and take them with all that risk, "and why she is doing that on her own without accessing good medical care."

There was considerable interest in the work of the Committee. There was a large increase in web traffic for the live streaming on the Oireachtas website, and there was also huge social media traffic surrounding it. Orla said the level of outside engagement with the Committee was clear from early on. NWCI could see that from its own social media stats as it and Lawyers for Choice live-tweeted many of the meetings.

From the beginning it was clear that Chairperson Senator Noone would be challenged at every turn by Deputy McGrath and Senator Mullen. She took to ensuring she had someone walking beside her as she left the committee room after finding herself involved in a row with Senator Mullen in the corridor one day. The exchange was reported in *The Times (Ireland Edition)* in October by Ellen Coyne, who wrote that a journalist and some TDs who were in the women's toilet outside the committee room at the time were able to overhear the entire exchange. Senator Mullen was upset after he was criticised for the way in which he questioned two representatives of the World Health Organisation (WHO) during his six minutes of questioning.

For the Committee members who were favourably disposed towards change, the Coalition to Repeal the Eighth Amendment, NWCI, Amnesty International Ireland, the Irish Family Planning Association and Doctors for Choice all worked to help provide them with information on abortion. For instance, how it was made available in other countries or pointing to research that had already been conducted on certain issues such as abortion pills. As Ailbhe explained:

"That is the perfectly legitimate work of civil society responding to requests for information. The Coalition's lobbying skills were

> well-honed at that stage and the National Women's Council were in constant communication with the members. We all worked very hard on that. Terminations for Medical Reasons were excellent and crucial throughout, as were Doctors for Choice. There was also a close interaction between the pro-Repeal TDs and the broad Repeal movement."

There were a number of explicitly pro-Repeal politicians, mainly women, on the Committee, such as Sinn Féin's health spokeswoman, Louise O'Reilly; People Before Profit TD Bríd Smith; Solidarity's Ruth Coppinger TD; independent Senator Lynn Ruane; Labour TD Jan O'Sullivan; Kate O'Connell TD of Fine Gael; and Independents 4 Change TD Clare Daly.

Several male politicians thought along similar lines, including Sinn Féin Senator Paul Gavan, and also Jonathan O'Brien TD, who had struggled with the issue at the start. This was to set a constructive tone for the Dáil debate, as the workings of the Committee were closely followed.

Deputy Billy Kelleher emerged as a strong spokesperson for moderate legislation, along with his party colleague Lisa Chambers, which wasn't easy for them in Fianna Fáil. There was a very powerful moment when Billy Kelleher spoke and said, "Picture a young girl alone in her room, about to take the abortion pill." Their colleague Senator Ned O'Sullivan was the surprise feminist on the Committee. He took on Rónán Mullen and Mattie McGrath, telling them: "If you start saying you're against contraception, you have no idea of what goes on in the real world and you are dinosaurs."

The behaviour of Deputy McGrath and Senator Mullin was viewed by many as obstreperous, as well as baffling because it was viewed as so extreme as to be alienating. "It's a democracy," said Ailbhe. "People are absolutely entitled to express their views. But when those views are based on very questionable facts or are down-right wrong, they have to be challenged and corrected." Despite the toughness of the Committee members' task, the deliberations were made easier by the clarity of the evidence from a number of the experts the Committee invited to speak.

Professor Sir Sabaratnam Arulkumaran, who chaired the HSE inquiry into the death of Savita Halappanavar, and is a former president of the Royal College of Obstetricians and Gynaecologists in the UK, had little time for the official Irish approach to abortion. He pointed out that making abortion illegal served only to promote illegal abortions. He referred to the fourteen-year prison sentence for any woman or girl who accessed an illegal abortion here, as provided for in the Protection of Life During Pregnancy Act, asking: "Can you imagine putting those 4,800 women in prison?"

The evidence on rape and incest, and how it was simply not possible to legislate for abortion in such cases, was quite clear. In the words of Assistant Professor of Law at Trinity College Dublin Dr David Kenny, it would be "unworkable". Tom O'Malley, senior law lecturer in NUI Galway, told the politicians "nothing short of a criminal conviction by a court would suffice to prove that the rape has been committed". But such legislative difficulties would be avoided in the "event that abortion was freely available for the first three months or whatever the period may be". Noeline Blackwell, CEO of the Dublin Rape Crisis Centre, made very clear the immense difficulties for women to report rapes. The discussion of rape was very significant in Orla's view:

"While at one level it was disturbing to listen to the members discuss the possibility of rape being a ground for abortion, of what criteria could be set to enable a doctor sign-off for termination for rape – it became very clear after this discussion that the majority of members, particularly those still forming their view, wanted to support women who were raped and the only way to do that would be to provide a period of on-request [abortion] where no reason was required. After that meeting I felt very confident that the Oireachtas Committee would decide to propose a period of on request. The question then was for how many weeks".

The Committee was subject to criticism for not being balanced in its list of witnesses in terms of presenting both sides of the abortion argument. Then Sinn Féin TD Peadar Tóibín, who was suspended from the parliamentary party for six months in 2013 when he voted against the Protection of Life During Pregnancy bill, and who eventually left the party over the issue, was critical of the number of witnesses favouring repeal of the amendment compared to the numbers of those in favour of retention.

But his then party colleague Jonathan O'Brien rejected the assertion. "The imbalance has been caused by pro-life groups refusing to appear before the Committee. Don't cry over spilt milk when you intentionally spilt it yourself just so you can cry", Mr O'Brien responded in a tweet.

That December, as the rest of the political world was beginning to wind down for Christmas, the Committee spent over three hours voting on individual recommendations, beginning with the question on repeal of the Eighth Amendment, which was proposed by Labour TD Jan O'Sullivan and passed overwhelmingly with the support of thirteen other members. Six members of the Committee voted against the measure. Catherine Noone abstained.

The second motion allowed for terminations where the life or the health of the woman is at risk without any distinction being drawn between the physical and mental health of the woman. Two physicians would be asked to determine whether an abortion should be provided. Gestational time limits for terminations would be guided by best medical advice and provided for in law. Six members voted against such a proposal; fourteen backed it. Catherine Noone abstained.

Then in a game-changing motion, Fianna Fáil TD Billy Kelleher proposed a motion, along with party colleagues Lisa Chambers TD and Senator Ned O'Sullivan, to allow for terminations without restriction up to twelve weeks. Their motion said this was in view of the complexities of legislating for the termination of pregnancy for reasons of rape and incest, that it would be more appropriate to deal with the issue by making the termination of pregnancy lawful with no restriction as to reason, up to a gestational limit of up to twelve weeks, through a GP-led service or delivered in a clinical context. The Committee passed that Fianna Fáil motion by twelve votes to five. During its series of votes, the Committee agreed to a number of changes to our abortion laws, including that access to terminations should be permitted when a mother's life, health or mental health is at risk. The Committee also voted on the individual recommendations of the Citizens' Assembly.

In the cases of fatal foetal abnormalities, eighteen members of the Committee supported terminations in these instances. Catherine Noone did cast her vote on that occasion, as she said she felt very strongly about this instance.

However a vote to allow for terminations in cases of non-fatal foetal abnormalities was rejected, as was a proposal to allow terminations for socioeconomic reasons. These were the only two Citizens' Assembly recommendations rejected by the Committee. Independent Senator Lynn Ruane, with the support of People Before Profit TD Bríd Smith, proposed allowing terminations with no restriction as to reason up to 22 weeks. Fine Gael TD Kate O'Connell and Independents 4 Change TD Clare Daly backed the recommendation, but the rest of the Committee voted against it.

There was disappointment in the ranks at this failure to get the socioeconomic proposals passed but Ailbhe said it was not a huge surprise, although she thought it was a great shame. The need to decriminalise abortion received widespread acceptance, with eighteen members supporting a proposal on this measure by Social Democrats TD Catherine Murphy. All members except Rónán Mullen, Mattie McGrath and Fine Gael TD Peter Fitzpatrick gave their approval to proposals to improve sex education in schools and provide free contraception.

Gráinne said ARC had been wary the Committee would be used as a way to water down the progressive positions the Citizens' Assembly had adopted:

> "That was how it was seen at the start and that was what it did in part. The Citizens' Assembly had recommended access on socioeconomic grounds up to 22 weeks. Despite the changes, the outcomes from the Committee far exceeded our expectations."

While it was all quite low-key, those votes felt like yet another significant step forward for Irish women's reproductive rights. Ailbhe explained:

> "You now had that double-whammy effect of the Assembly and the Committee, as it went into the Oireachtas, of this having been given a lot of thought, a lot of attention, a lot of consideration. Nobody could say that this had not been thoroughly debated and discussed."

Yet the doubts about an abortion referendum happening never disappeared. Oireachtas members reported feeling very pressurised and being canvassed strongly by colleagues on both sides as they all watched the Committee appear to go on a similar 'journey' over its three-month timeframe as the Citizens' Assembly had done before it. Given that the Government was in a confidence and supply arrangement with Fianna Fáil would there be enough votes in favour to carry a proposal for a referendum? The Fianna Fáil members on the Committee had shown real leadership, but it remained to be seen how many they were leading in their own party. Party leader Micheál Martin was another unknown quantity.

Gauging Fine Gael members, even the Cabinet members, was not straightforward either. It was known that Tánaiste Simon Coveney would not be comfortable with twelve weeks without restriction. All the while though, the politicians were seeing how the opinion polls were consistently showing that voters wanted the Eighth Amendment repealed.

While the Committee was conducting its hearings Orla decided in November it would be timely for NWCI to publish a document it had been working on. In advance of the launch she approached the political editor of the *Irish Times*, Pat Leahy, who wrote an article saying NWCI, the largest representative organisation for women in Ireland, would launch a campaign that week to appeal to the 'middle ground' in the abortion debate. The 'Every Woman' campaign would adopt new language and focus on women's needs and the realities of their lives, according to people familiar with it, read the article:

"It will seek the repeal of the Eighth Amendment and legislation which permits abortion on request in the early part of pregnancy. In the later part of pregnancy – after 12–14 weeks – the council will seek access to abortion on health grounds, and where the pregnancy is 'non-viable'."

Orla was quoted as saying the main thing for NWCI was to reflect the conversations they'd been having with women over the last year: "For women it's not a political issue. It's a personal and private one."

She remembers being exceptionally nervous in advance of the publication of 'Every Woman' but one of the things that had happened after the NWCI presentation at the Citizens' Assembly was that it was agreed there needed to be more leadership in terms of that middle ground and communicating the issue of abortion to those who were uncomfortable about talking and thinking about it.

There was constant discussion in NWCI on how a new way needed to be found to talk about the issue of abortion – how to create a space where women and men could share their views, ask questions, and recount their own experiences and concerns in a non-judgemental and non-threatening space.

To facilitate that, NWCI organised a series of 'open conversations' nationwide engaging people whose minds were not made up on abortion, who said they had reservations about abortions but primarily wanted a safe space to talk. They used an independent facilitator. "This was a new type of undertaking for NWCI as there was no advocacy element to the conversations. Participants were encouraged to explore their knowledge of and views on abortion", explained Orla, adding that the public response to these 'open conversations' was enormous and so positive that these public meetings continued to be held around the country including during the referendum campaign. In the first five months of 2018 NWCI held over 25 small and large conversations in almost every county in Ireland.

NWCI had been involved in the focus group research process commissioned by the Coalition, along with ARC, Amnesty International Ireland, the Irish Family Planning Association and the Irish

Council for Civil Liberties, which highlighted these sorts of findings. It was understood there was a serious gap between public understanding of the issues and the tired debates that dominated politics and the media. NWCI had engaged Adam May, director of the advertising and design agency Language, who had been working closely with the Coalition since 2015, to assist in developing this new initiative. As Orla explained:

> "The language and values in 'Every Woman' was new with regards to abortion; while its essence was articulating the same outcomes for women, it was placing abortion within a woman's health context rather than a human rights framework. This approach was seen as controversial by some commentators and activists but we were confident it was necessary to engage and include the broadest range of people in the conversation. ... The response was so positive from our members, from politicians, it gave them a new way of speaking about abortion and also within a wider context that they felt comfortable to engage in. It filled a vacuum that was there for people in the middle who the research showed us could go either way when it came to voting. The values, messages, language of NWCI 'Every Woman' became core to Together for Yes."

On the basis of participants' questions and comments during those open conversations, NWCI developed a booklet that addressed some of the frequently asked questions.

Meanwhile ARC concentrated its efforts on a 'Talk to Your TD' initiative, urging people to go to constituency clinics of TDs and talk "about why Free, Safe, Legal matters to you". The responses of the various TDs would be fed back centrally for analysis. Furthering the preparation for a referendum, in 2016 the group was also training people on how to speak about abortion, running training courses around the country through local groups which had been established. It also delivered 'values clarification training', which was based on training from Catholics for Choice, a US pro-choice Catholic advocacy group. This group states that it gives training on how to advocate on reproductive issues with sensitivity and confidence and to "use value and ethical arguments to successfully counter opposition and gain new support" as well as "grapple honestly with ethical, moral and social tensions". It also aims to gain the upper hand in media and debates. As Gráinne explained:

> "We changed the title from 'Values Clarification' to 'Conversations about Choice'. But they were essentially workshops that supported people to explore what they thought about abortion and why we think the way we do. It really helped people to identify their own biases and to be able to have frank conversations about abortion. It's a stigma reduction tool and it's about helping people to understand why we propose free, safe and legal. Most people when they come to ARC are instinctively pro-choice or have come to that point through experience but haven't worked out their position in detail. They're interested, they're sympathetic but they haven't fully worked through what values motivate their position. I remember working through those issues myself when first presented with concepts like gender-selective abortion. The silence around abortion in Ireland meant a lack of information and even conversation about issues like gender-selective or late-term abortion. But from tracking debate internationally, we knew that these issues would likely be raised by the other side during a referendum campaign so we needed to fully understand them to know where we stood and ensure we could respond."

The Coalition to Repeal the Eighth Amendment also had very valuable support from Catholics for Choice, which meant that it was also able to subsequently provide both values clarification and media and communications training for its members nationally.

The final report of the Oireachtas Committee on the Eighth Amendment of the Constitution was published on 20 December 2017 and sent to the Oireachtas for consideration. Hardly Yuletide reading but over that Christmas period everyone from the Taoiseach down needed to decide exactly where they stood on the issue and what the Government was now going to propose.

7

Building a Unified Campaign

~~~~~~

Into that difficult mix of pushing for a referendum, preparing for one, and attempting to build as solid a base of unity as possible, was the highly contentious issue of tone. Its use, or urgings that it might be taken into consideration, pushed a red button of rage for many people. It did not feel like a coincidence that an almost overwhelmingly female campaign was being described as shrill and strident.

Given Ireland's history of control and punishment when it came to female reproductive issues, the emotion and outrage was understandable. In an article on the *Headstuff* website in August 2017, Tara

Flynn was quoted as saying that tone policing was a huge problem for the Repeal campaign, particularly in relation to Irish media. The "bounds of politeness" she argued, could only be stretched so far when misinformation is being so readily spread, and members of the movement are being lied about and stigmatised. "(The media) start writing things like 'I think the Repeal campaign should mind its manners', when we've been minding it against all odds and all kinds of attacks", she says. "Sometimes we get angry, and guess what – we're allowed to get angry."

In the same article Linda Kavanagh of ARC said it was opinion pieces and columns in mainstream press rather than on social media sites where pro-choice activism was described as "shrill" and "extreme".

"It appears that most of the authors of these opinion pieces believe the accusation to be so self-evident that further corroboration is not required," she said.

They do not specify who they mean, she said. "It could be the case that some commentators are reacting to things people say on Twitter … but people on Twitter are usually commenting in their capacity as private citizens. We can't be held responsible for the opinions of random people."

Opinion columnist Una Mullally wrote in the *Irish Times* in September 2016 that as the movement for abortion rights in Ireland grows, there was an increasing and predictable irritation with the 'tone' of the movement: too strident, too shrill, too demanding, too confrontational. "Why can't we be quiet about women's rights so as not to offend or irritate? Because being mute doesn't get you heard", wrote Mullally.

But advice on watching tone would come from unexpected quarters. Rory O'Neill, aka Panti Bliss, advised the pro-choice campaigners that when passion turns to anger, as it all too easily can, that puts people off and the abortion referendum would not be gay marriage part two. Those who want the legislation changed must include everyone in a cool-headed 'national conversation' about abortion:

"There is a time and a place for righteous anger – and I am not saying everyone should be meek – but you need to think strategically when it comes to referendums. Sometimes you might want to stand up and scream your head off, but not when you are trying to speak to the middle ground. When it comes to abortion, it's sometimes forgotten that you can give someone all the facts as you see them but you won't change a mind that believes abortion is murder. They are not misogynists or monsters for [believing] that."

Ailbhe sighs in memory at the difficulties of keeping the Coalition to Repeal the Eighth Amendment together throughout this time:

"I have never done anything as difficult in my life. The monthly meetings could be very tough. I would be there with Sinéad [Kennedy] beside me, which was fantastic because I couldn't have done it without her. There was never any shouting but it was robust argument. Some felt that we should have a very strong argument effectively about choice and human rights, while others thought that you can come at it another way, which is to stress the plain reality of abortion in this country.

We had to recognise that how we interacted with people had to be different, had to be calm. Of course it was about public perception. We knew that people were uncomfortable with the word 'abortion', and that for them 'pro-choice' signalled 'radical' and even 'extreme'. One of the reasons why I wanted us to do research, as soon as possible, was so that we would be clear about what people were actually thinking, and that did happen. We gradually worked through the difference of approach and position in a very practical, nitty-gritty way, becoming step by step a more unified campaign. We also had to centre and give more spine to our social media work. Coming up to the Citizens' Assembly, we stressed that it was very important not to be over-reactive because the other side simply retaliate in force and amplify the divide, and that we

> could not allow ourselves to be provoked into distracting arguments, however upset and offended we were."

While each side was busy preparing for the looming referendum, there was no escaping the sense that the mother of all battles was on the horizon. Nerves had been further frayed before Christmas when a controversy involving then Tánaiste Frances Fitzgerald had threatened to bring down the Government and cause a general election. Where would that leave a referendum? In the event, she resigned from Government. Ironically, she would have been an early supporter of the need to liberalise our abortion laws and exerted steady pressure on the issue around the Cabinet table.

During the summer of 2017, Ailbhe and Orla had been working with Colm O'Gorman of Amnesty International Ireland on possible campaign structures ahead of a referendum. There was a lot of hard talking done to try to make sure they were all on the same page. Eilís Ní Chaithnía, policy officer with NWCI, was working with Orla to develop possible campaign structures. Later on, ARC was invited into the conversation, as were the Union of Students in Ireland, the Irish Family Planning Association and the Irish Council for Civil Liberties.

In mid-2017, Gráinne was active on the ARC board and following the AGM in November 2017, with the referendum looming, she stepped in to support the new convenors, Sarah Monaghan and Denise O'Toole, with the pre-referendum discussions. However when she did she was dismayed with what she saw as the level of disarray and disagreement among the groups. At that point meetings were taking place in a large building on Upper Mount Street arranged by ARC. Trust levels were very low, she felt, and the atmosphere at times "toxic".

ARC were on good terms with all of the parties but it was clear that all the NGOs in the room were not in the process of coming together in a shared campaign leadership. It wasn't working. ARC volunteers found the situation difficult to swallow as it appeared that differences between individuals were going to jeopardise the referendum campaign they had fought so hard for.

Orla had her own frustrations at this time:

> "There was a lot of – I think – of historical baggage between some organisations, different styles of working and also perceptions and understandings of campaigning. It was a bit of a melting pot. So we were certainly not at the point of 'what are the messages of the campaign' then; we were just trying to work out how to best work together. This was all going on in the six months up to Christmas."

She remembered one particular occasion, a relatively simple episode, which served to clarify to her that too many groups trying to work together was simply too difficult and unwieldy, not to mention time-consuming.

> "It was agreed to send a joint letter to the Oireachtas Committee on the Eighth Amendment. It took a week to agree, with many back-and-forth emails and phone calls; it became clear to me and Ailbhe that we couldn't continue working in this way and be effective in a referendum campaign. It was a real concern that in December we were entering a critical period before the referendum and the focus was still on the processes rather than what we were trying to achieve."

Orla and NWCI Chairperson Ellen O'Malley Dunlop then stood back and looked at who, in an ideal world, they would work well with in a campaign. "We really narrowed it down, because working with so many organisations in terms of a campaign structure – well we just couldn't see it working."

Looking at the cold hard facts, Orla decided that it was best for NWCI to work with Ailbhe and the Coalition and found that Ailbhe had come to the same conclusion:

> "It wasn't easy but I just thought it has to be Ailbhe, and the Coalition. Ailbhe is so identified with the issue of the Eighth and NWCI was one of the founding members of the Coalition. We

> always had a good relationship and since I became director of NWCI Ailbhe was always a person who would give me great objective advice; I knew we could work together under pressure."

So then before Christmas Orla met with Ellen O'Malley Dunlop and they proposed to the NWCI board that Orla would go to Ailbhe and they would look at how the Coalition and NWCI could form a referendum campaign. Subsequently, Ailbhe put it to some key people in the Coalition. She came back to Orla and said she felt it would absolutely need to involve the Abortion Rights Campaign:

> "Initially I was nervous about ARC and I knew members of NWCI were because we felt the campaign needed to focus on the people who were undecided and unsure of the issue of abortion in order to mobilise enough people to vote Yes. We didn't know if ARC would also be of that view. Our thinking was that ARC will speak to the converted and we needed a campaign that was going to speak to all those people whose minds were not made up."

ARC wanted to be a part of that core leadership group. In fact they were quite determined to be in it. They recognised, Gráinne said, that Ailbhe and Orla were going to work together and that both of their organisations had important roles to play. The board of ARC had met and decided to put together a proposal to join them at the leadership table, even though they knew it would involve considerable compromise on their part:

> "We also decided that the referendum campaign wouldn't work without us because we were the only ones with grassroots activists, and the only ones with any money. We had a reach across thousands of activists. We had a large formal membership but we also had a much wider reach with our networks and social media, for example there were hundreds of people who raised money for ARC through the Workers Beer Company every

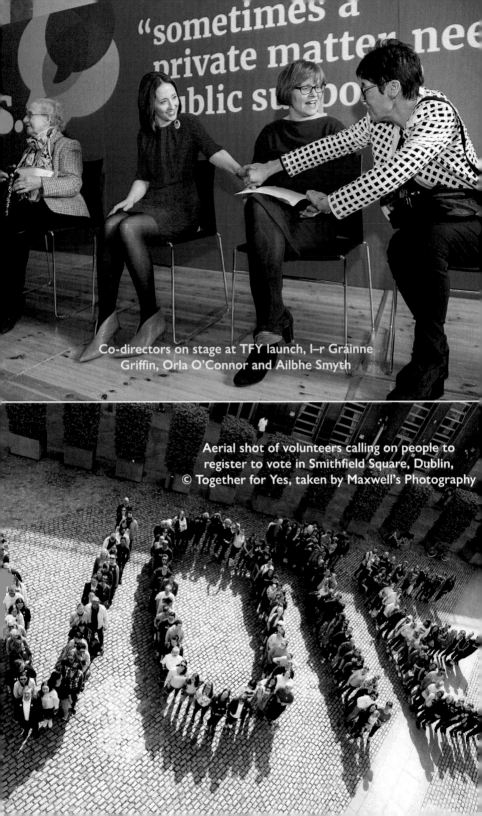

Co-directors on stage at TFY launch, l–r Gráinne Griffin, Orla O'Connor and Ailbhe Smyth

Aerial shot of volunteers calling on people to register to vote in Smithfield Square, Dublin, © Together for Yes, taken by Maxwell's Photography

'She lives on your street' photoshoot in Phibsborough, Dublin

Poster launch outside TFY's Mount Street HQ, © Together for Yes, taken by Maxwell's Photography

On the canvass in Maynooth, Co. Kildare

'Get Together for Yes' regional tour in Cork, © Barry Cronin

A street stall in Spiddal, Co. Galway, © Barry Cronin

Getting Together for Yes in Gorey,
Co. Wexford, © Barry Cronin

The TFY roadshow in Ennis, Co. Clare,
© Barry Cronin

Waterford TFY activists walking in her shoes
(and the rain) at the bus station on the quay

Offaly TFY activists in Tullamore

Donegal TFY activists in Malin Head the evening before the vote, © Bauke Roof

Joanna Hickey, Kellie Sweeney, Susan Roche and Rachel Egan relaxing between shots at Nurses for Yes photo shoot, © Aileen O'Carroll

Senior female obstetricians join with Midwives Together for Yes and Minister for Health Simon Harris to canvass match-goers ahead of the Leinster v Munster rugby match, © Together for Yes, taken by Maxwell's Photography

Volunteers Ciara Browne, Eoin Madsen and Anna Carnegie packing boxes of campaign literature in TFY HQ, © Derek Speirs

Amy Rose Harte addressing the daily HQ team meeting on 23 May, © Derek Speirs

The morning of the vote (l–r Deirdre Duffy, Karl Hayden, Orla O'Connor, Gráinne Griffin and Ailbhe Smyth), © Aileen O'Carroll

Dublin North-West TFY at RDS count centre

Members of the HQ team on stage at Dublin Castle (l–r Orla Howard, Sinéad Kennedy, Ailbhe Smyth, Orla O'Connor, Gráinne Griffin, Sarah Monaghan, Deirdre Duffy), © Derek Speirs

'Ireland has lit a beacon of hope': co-directors at press conference on 27 May, © Caroline Quinn

Activists pay tribute at the mural in memory of Savita Halappanavar, © Derek Speirs

> summer and loads of people who would come to clothes swaps and other Repeal-themed social events even if they never went to meetings."

So ARC wrote a pitch outlining why they should be part of the leadership of the referendum campaign, which included a risk analysis and statement of core principles. Gráinne and Sarah Monaghan, who was ARC co-convenor at that time, sought a meeting with Orla and Ailbhe to put forward their proposal. "We said we think you're setting up a referendum campaign. We want to be part of the campaign. We want to be fully at the table with an equal say. This is what we can bring."

A meeting was arranged between the four women and Orla said she laid out her concerns around the messaging of the campaign:

> "I said, 'I think we are saying different things'. So we agreed to have a meeting where we would thrash out the messaging. Adam May presented the messaging that had been developed from the research. It was the messaging similar to what we had worked on in 'Every Woman', the health-based messaging. We had this long meeting where we discussed each value and core message. It was one of the most important meetings because we went through everything and we now had a strong sense and understanding of where we were all coming from and what was important to each of us. We developed a trust between us that would carry through into the campaign."

ARC had pitched their co-convenor Sarah Monaghan as campaign co-director, along with Orla and Ailbhe. Gráinne and Sarah approached the ARC leadership of the referendum campaign as a partnership between the two of them. Sarah was leaving her job in restaurant management and was in a position at that point to work full-time on the campaign and to have a media profile. But Ailbhe and Orla, while responding positively to ARC's pitch, did have a proviso – they wanted one director from each organisation, and because of the longer developed relationship with Gráinne wanted

Marino Branch
Brainse Marino
Tel: 8336297

Gráinne to be the co-director from ARC, with Sarah Monaghan joining the campaign executive. But being asked to be a co-director was not ideal for Gráinne, a manager in the public sector. She would be limited in what leave she could take and there would be restrictions on public engagement. She agreed to take up the role, but she would not act in a public-facing capacity or be a media spokesperson. Sarah Monaghan would do media work instead while Gráinne deleted her LinkedIn account and minimised her profile where she could. These stipulations were agreed with the other co-directors and ARC before she took up the role.

The agreement was reached that if the three groups came together their campaign would stand over the Oireachtas Committee recommendations. "So that's what moved it, that gave it a framework", said Gráinne. ARC also added, with the others in full agreement, that the campaign would rely on evidence-based messaging and as far as possible be inclusive of minority voices and that it wouldn't be discriminatory. An ARC EGM was called in early February, lasting a full day. Sarah Monaghan remembers feeling "terrified" ahead of it. As co-convenor she did much of the presenting that day explaining why ARC should join this new platform with the Coalition to Repeal the Eighth Amendment and NWCI. She recognised it as a hugely important meeting. She remembered saying to Gráinne that morning that if the eventual vote turned out to be something like 51 per cent she did not know would she able to lead on such a low approval rating, with only half the membership behind them. Sarah recalled:

"We just opened it up. You know we put it all out, all that intensive work we had put in beforehand. We put everything we could think of, any possible scenario that we could think of, on the table. Then we heard all the issues, all the criticisms, all the fears. We explained how it might work, how ARC might take a seat at the table, what that would look like, what we needed it to look like, what we thought our members might need it to look like. We said these are the risks of doing it, these are the risks of not doing it, this is what we're likely to be rolling out in terms of messaging and language and it's going to be more conservative, it's going to be softer, it's going be middle ground. So I suppose we were saying that there will be compromises necessary here and they will be uncomfortable to a lot of you. Can we suck it up for the greater good? And I suppose that was really at the root of it.

I suppose it just kept coming back around to what if we don't, what if we don't join it? What if we try to run some parallel campaign. We're just strengthening the chances that we will lose here. And then what do we do? It's all been for nothing, and we've let women down. There are women relying on us now to get this campaign across the final hurdle. And we just can't let our own egos, our even morals, kind of cloud that. There's just a bigger picture here. So you know everyone in that room, and everyone who had been a member for so long, they did a lot of compromise on the campaign that they would have liked to see. They just faced what the reality was, that we were now pitching to a different audience. It was a terrifying experience, truth be told, for me and I'm sure for Gráinne as well.

This is an organisation we've so much love for, so much belief in, that had brought us so far. And I suppose one of the first things was acknowledging for all of them that we wouldn't be here without them, we wouldn't be there without their work on the ground for so long, committed to an issue then that no one cared about. But now we were there we needed to move into something different. And you know the vote was unanimous: 100 per cent yes vote. It taught me a lot about trusting in your membership. If anything for me it reaffirmed why we organise in the way that we do; that is the benefit of being non-hierarchical. You have full communication, but you also have fully committed and well-rounded intelligent members who understand the complexities and when given the chance are able to embrace it and make the right decision.

And so that to me was a very special part of the campaign. It's something that often campaigns I think fail to do is bring the base into a more mainstream campaign. I'm sure you could

> see that on the other side. They just failed to compromise. They couldn't hold it together; they couldn't pretend that they thought it was OK in a situation of rape. They just couldn't do it."

Orla remembers being very impressed with how ARC pulled it all together:

> "So they came back fully behind the values and messaging. Gráinne's line to people was 'suck it up': you mightn't like it but we're going to win this referendum. And the relationship subsequently between NWCI and ARC and the staff in both was just brilliant. It was the really honest conversations around our thinking and our differences and how we all wanted to achieve the same result that brought us together."

The three co-directors are united in the belief that a very tough aspect of the preparation and the decision for their organisations to join together was in not including other organisations such as Amnesty International Ireland and the Union of Students in Ireland. The co-directors believed they could work well together on a personal level and that this was true also for their organisations. "It was a really difficult decision going to the other organisations and saying we're doing this ourselves. It was a very difficult time", said Orla.

Gráinne also has regrets over some of the fallout from what she saw as necessary decisions. But she is pragmatic about it. "There were too many people around the table and it wasn't coming together. It was never going to get to a point where there was a unified campaign with seven directors around the table. Something was going to have to give."

The importance of personal relationships was a big factor for Orla. "It was so important that me and Ailbhe and Gráinne got on, so in some ways it probably wouldn't have worked with more. And if the leaders aren't working well together, nothing's working together – even in terms of just the logistics."

Ailbhe also acknowledged there was annoyance at how things turned out:

> "I understand that these kinds of things happen in campaigns because there's a lot at stake for people. But it was absolutely the right decision for us. It was a pragmatic decision made by three organisations that had been solidly working together since the end of 2013, all founding members of the Coalition to Repeal the Eighth Amendment. I had a very sticky meeting of the coalition steering group but basically banged the table and said this was the only way to go. I pointed out that although some people weren't happy with the decision to join up with ARC and NWCI to create this new campaign organisation, the majority were. I ended up saying we had a campaign to run and those who agree are in, and those who are not are not. In the end nobody actually bailed."

A number of meetings between the Together for Yes co-directors, as well as Sinéad Kennedy from the Coalition, Silke Paasche from NWCI and Sarah Monaghan from ARC, were facilitated by Aoife Dermody. This was done in order to work out a leadership structure, and the various strands of the campaign which would prove to be key preparatory work ahead of the intensity of a campaign. Given the difference in culture and approaches, not to have done so would have been a disaster in terms of presenting a unified campaign.

NWCI and ARC were very different in terms of structure: one an NGO with salaried staff and in receipt of government funding, the other an entirely voluntary organisation, with hundreds of members, each with an equal say. Gráinne explained:

> "We had been building relationships with all those organisations over the years but it was difficult at times because of the fact that our representatives would change. It was also practically very difficult for ARC members to consistently engage with NGOs long-term as most ARC members worked in full-time jobs and had to take annual leave to go to meetings during the day."

Her ARC colleague Sarah Monaghan remembers this as being a really intense time. Now working as a campaign strategist, she was managing restaurants then:

> "I was living ARC. I was working over 40/50 hours a week at the restaurant job and then spending all the time outside of that working on ARC stuff. So generally I would leave work and go straight to the office and work there. For a period of time in January we were all in there. We might as well have moved into our offices; we were all there till 2 a.m. every night."

It was also a challenging time for NWCI as due to the constraints of no State funding for referendums all the NWCI staff working on the campaign had to work a significant time in a voluntary capacity. As time went on more meetings were held and Orla and Gráinne developed a close working relationship. "In the end Gráinne and my working style were often more similar than Ailbhe's and we had more common ground in terms of pitching the campaign message", recalled Orla. However Gráinne wasn't the leader of ARC because ARC did not have a leader. It was all far from straightforward.

Once the New Year had arrived Ailbhe said they all recognised they were now "in referendum territory":

> "So everything you do, absolutely every step you take, every flick of an eyelash, is about a referendum. We didn't have a date but it was coming, which meant that you have to be entirely focused on the voters. You are always conscious, if you are in any kind of leadership position, which the three of us were, that everything you do will be noticed by a voter somewhere and it will get out there. You have to be intensely political and pragmatic and focused, the whole time. There was no time for Christmas, no time for anything except the referendum. The question all the time is: what is going to work here? What is needed? We were thinking about the money and how we were going to fund the campaign. Who are we going to draw in to work with us on specific fronts?"

There was, she said, "a lot of hard talking with the Abortion Rights Campaign to make sure that we were all on the same page."

> "We were also talking with the Union of Students in Ireland [USI], who may have felt disappointed that ultimately they weren't centrally involved in the leadership. That was nothing against USI, rather our sense that USI always run a good referendum campaign themselves. They know how to mobilise the students. And they'd been very involved in Register to Vote. We worked very well with USI subsequently and they did a fantastic job.
>
> At that stage, I was certainly thinking all the time about how we could move forward. You can't relax because you're on high alert. You're thinking 'get me out of this meeting, it's wasting my time.' You're building up your troops, and that's what we were doing in the Coalition, working to get everyone on board, and on more or less the same wavelength."

By the middle of January Taoiseach Leo Varadkar was still playing his cards close to his chest and declining to give his views on the report of the Oireachtas Committee on the Eighth, which recommended legislating for abortion on request up to twelve weeks. Fianna Fáil was the second biggest party in the Dáil and although considerable effort had been put in by a number of organisations to try to bring as many of that party's TDs as possible around to a liberal position on abortion it was an uphill battle. Party leader Micheál Martin was known as being socially conservative.

The Fianna Fáil leader had begun a segment of an interview in April 2017 on local radio station KFM on abortion by saying that he came from "a pro-life disposition". The exchange with presenter Shane Beatty became tense when Micheál Martin was asked whether he would support abortion in cases of incest, for instance if someone was raped by their father and became pregnant as a result. He replied, "It's not that simple, it's just not that simple." It depended, he added, on a number of issues. "I know people today who are alive through their mother being raped. In one particular case she was the outcome of that and she gets very angry when people suggest she should never have had a life. This is not simple, and I think it's an issue that'll come before the Oireachtas."

But just nine months after that radio interview the Fianna Fáil leader would cause shock and joy when he stood in the Dáil to make his contribution to a debate on the Oireachtas Committee on the Eighth Amendment report. Micheál Martin's speech took place early in the debate and followed a parliamentary party meeting where a majority of party members present had spoken against the prospect of repealing the Eighth Amendment.

Mr Martin began by saying the debate was first and foremost an opportunity for each deputy to explain how they were going to approach the fundamental decisions which must be taken in the months ahead. Abortion is not an issue where a unanimous opinion is possible, said the Corkman. Radically opposed opinions on this issue are held with great passion, conviction and sincerity. A basic challenge for us, he said, was to do everything possible to enable a respectful debate:

> "Over the years I have been on the record as being against a significant change in our abortion laws. I have done so from a belief that this was the most effective way of affirming the importance of the unborn. While I have supported different proposals to clarify the law and to address the threat to the life of the mother I have been broadly in favour of the law as enabled by the Eighth Amendment."

However, he continued, we each have a duty to be willing to question our own views, to be open to different perspectives and to respond to new information. On an issue as profoundly important as this we must all struggle with complex and discomforting medical and ethical issues. "If our views change, if the facts become clearer, if we come to understand properly the impact of a policy on others then we must be willing to act accordingly."

An increasing number of cases of abortions are happening in Ireland, he said, with the availability of pills which can cause an abortion in the first 70 days of a pregnancy being widespread and growing.

He then made his position absolutely clear, grounded in his concern for women. It was a jolt to those listening, including members of his own party who were not aware of what he had been going to say and were stunned.

"Because of these reasons and following a long period of reflection and assessment of evidence before the Oireachtas Committee, I believe that we should remove the Eighth Amendment from Bunreacht na hÉireann and I will vote accordingly."

As such, he supported the idea of a "time-based cut-off near the end of the first trimester". The move caused huge consternation among his own party ranks, but also in Fine Gael for different reasons. A number in that party believed the Fianna Fáil leader had stolen the political initiative from the Taoiseach.

Looking back, Orla, Ailbhe and Gráinne all felt that decision by the Fianna Fáil leader was a significant turning point in support being gained for the Repeal movement and more specifically the recommendations of the Oireachtas Committee on the Eighth Amendment.

Health Minister Simon Harris had opened that Dáil debate by bringing home how widespread the reality of abortion was in Ireland. He read into the record the number of women from each county in Ireland who had travelled to the UK in 2016.

Further pressing the message that women needing abortions come from every corner of the country, he pointed out that out of a total of 2,745 women the highest number, at 1,175, were women from Dublin and the lowest, 15, were women from Monaghan. Each county in between had varying numbers. "These are not faceless women. They are our friends and neighbours, sisters, cousins, mothers, aunts, wives."

Dispelling the myth of young, single women needing abortions, he pointed out that over half of the women who travelled were married, in a civil partnership, or in a relationship. The Minister said 85 per cent of the women were between three and twelve weeks pregnant. "I can't help but wonder what we would have done if we didn't have a neighbouring island to help us turn a blind eye. And sometimes turning a blind eye is the same as turning your back."

During his speech the Minister referenced the Magdalene laundries, mother and baby homes, the Kerry Babies case and the tragedy of Ann Lovett, a fifteen-year-old schoolgirl who died while giving birth beside a grotto in Co. Longford in 1984. He concluded by stating:

> "I do not doubt that, as long as I remain a member of this House, I will continue to witness moments in this Chamber that remind us of darker times in our history. But let this be a different type of moment. Let this be a moment people will look back on as one where their representatives confronted one of the most complex issues we have faced as a country with clarity, with compassion and with care."

One of the most notorious and shameful cases in Irish history – the Kerry Babies case – had just re-entered public debate at that time after Kerrywoman Joanne Hayes and her family had received an apology from An Garda Síochána for the ordeal they endured after the botched Garda investigation into the discovery of the body of a baby near Cahersiveen in April 1984.

Indeed in her contribution to the debate, Fine Gael TD Kate O'Connell said Ireland was at its least Christian point during its most Catholic years. She said the position of the Catholic Church had been sewn into the Constitution in 1937, two years after the sale, advertising and importation of contraceptives was banned. "Irish women were quite literally enslaved in an act of Church and State collusion that can be honestly characterised as nothing other than sexual apartheid." Their babies were sold like puppies to foreign homes or enslaved in industrial schools, she added, to be preyed upon by those in power wielding authority.

However, her colleague Minister of State John Paul Phelan gave a different view. Despite his name, he said, he was not a particularly Catholic person but he could not "ever support the conscious, purposeful destruction of a viable pregnancy". He did not believe a fertilised egg was a human being but the proposal that abortion should be available up to twelve weeks was not only unacceptable, "but I believe there is a considerable chance that if it was put to the general public, it would be defeated."

Kerry independent TD Michael Healy-Rae said he believed passionately in what he was about to say and it came from the way he was brought up. "I want to talk about the gift of life … I just don't agree with abortion. I believe it is always wrong." He spoke of a friend of his who, along with his sister, had been adopted and given the "gift of life". He said both his friends had a great life. "Who am I to deny these people the right to life? What right have I to do that?" he said.

His brother Deputy Danny Healy-Rae said he believed an abortion was "really hurtful. It is really so bad. What the abortionist does is inject the baby twice, first to paralyse it and then to stop the heartbeat. I believe that is murder."

Fianna Fáil Sligo–Leitrim–South-Donegal–North-Roscommon TD Eamon Scanlon said that "as a father I feel that the best way I could properly love and support my daughter or any other relation or friend in crisis pregnancy is if I also supported the little child that she was carrying." But overall that Dáil debate was strongly pro-repeal.

Subsequent to that debate the first Cabinet meeting of 2017, lasting four hours, would be dominated by a discussion of abortion. Afterwards, in a late-night press conference in Government Buildings, the Taoiseach, clearly nursing a head cold, announced that formal approval had been given to the holding of a referendum on abortion in late May or early June. We know, he said, that many women are obtaining abortion pills through the post to end their pregnancies, without any medical support, or counselling, or supervision. He continued:

> "I believe this is a decision about whether we want to continue to stigmatise and criminalise our sisters, our co-workers, and our friends. Or whether we are prepared to make a collective act of leadership to show empathy and compassion."

The amendment proposed, if approved by the people, would delete Article 40.3.3 in its entirety and remove the effective constitutional ban on abortion from the Constitution. It would repeal the Eighth Amendment and the thirteenth and fourteenth amendments linked to it, as well as inserting a new clause confirming that the Oireachtas may provide for the termination of pregnancies in accordance with law. This was being done on the advice of the Attorney General, and would give assurance that the Oireachtas had the power to legislate, and to balance any rights or interests, without preventing or restricting access to the courts on a point of law.

The proposed legislation would be published prior to the referendum and would be in line with the recommendations of the Oireachtas Committee. If the amendment is approved in a referendum, he explained, abortion in Ireland will become "safe, legal and rare", in the situations provided for by the Oireachtas. If the referendum is defeated, the law will remain as it is now.

In his speech the Taoiseach said that on the matter of twelve weeks, as proposed by the Oireachtas Committee, people would have to make up their own minds, based on the evidence and their own conscience. He had had to think long and hard about the provision for abortion without a specific indication in those first twelve weeks. However the Oireachtas Committee had rightly pointed out the impossibility of requiring women to establish that their pregnancy was as a result of rape or incest. During subsequent questioning by journalists the Taoiseach did say that many politicians were concerned about that twelve-week proposal, worrying it might be "a step too far" for a lot of people. It went further than many people had anticipated and certainly further than he himself would have anticipated a year or two previously. To muddle things further, he added, "but then again perhaps not".

If the referendum was approved by the Irish people, a doctor-led, safe and legal system for the termination of pregnancies would be introduced. There would be restrictions. After twelve weeks' gestation, abortion would only be allowed in exceptional circumstances, such as a serious risk to the life or health of the woman or in the event of a fatal foetal abnormality. Ultimately, it would be a decision based on the wishes of the woman concerned and the best available medical evidence, a private and personal matter for women and doctors. "No more X Cases, C cases, Miss Ys or Miss A, Miss B, or Miss C", said the Taoiseach.

That phrase, 'a step too far', regarding that twelve weeks would be repeated often by a number of politicians in the following weeks, even those who had not yet made up their mind on where they stood. They were nervous at what they saw as the unrestricted access to abortion that far into pregnancy. This hit the nerves of the campaigning groups. While it may have made some sense politically for the Taoiseach to reflect the uncertainty felt by many in his own party, and wider, it continued the pattern whereby no one ever felt quite sure exactly where Leo Varadkar stood on the issue, and how far he would go to bat for his own Government's proposal.

Gráinne had always believed that a referendum would only be held once the levels of public and political pressure reached a critical mass:

> "That's what all the work was about, we needed to force it through, fight for it, make it an inevitability. We needed to make it something the Government did not have a way out of. They would never have delivered of their own accord. We had our allies like Deputies Clare Daly and Ruth Coppinger, the people who had been killing themselves for years to keep it on the agenda; there was just no doubt as to where they stood. It was the pressure from the UN. It was the domestic alliances and the building alliances with political parties and the backbenchers. It was the grassroots activism, the marches, the stigma reduction, giving a new generation of younger people, overwhelmingly women, a vocabulary and the permission to be loud and be proud and demand changes. It was about opening doors for these people to come forward. By the time the Government announced a referendum you couldn't go anywhere without falling over a Repeal jumper."

8

Raring to Go: A Referendum Is Called

~~~~~~

It's difficult now to imagine a campaign name other than 'Together for Yes', but in truth the name was contentious when first proposed and caused tensions. "We had so many conversations over the name", said Orla, remembering the real difficulties around the all-important campaign identity. But from the moment she heard 'Together for Yes' she believed it ticked all the boxes. "Myself and Silke [Paasche of NWCI] knew it had to be positive, a name that went beyond the current campaign to engage with more people."

Sinéad Kennedy, co-founder of the Coalition to Repeal the Eighth Amendment, remembers herself and Ailbhe not liking it at all. There was a lot of time spent arguing on it:

> "It's funny retrospectively when I think back. Ailbhe and I absolutely hated the name. None of us loved it, but I think we agreed on it because we couldn't come up with anything better. It sounded so bland and corporate. Some people wanted a more pro-choice name, like Yes for Choice or Together for Choice. But there were also a lot of people saying they didn't think people were quite there yet. That's why we ended up with Together for Yes.
>
> In some ways for everybody it became a question of default. We all realised that we had to come together to work together for a yes. So it made sense. Without liking it we all got behind it. The interesting thing is that by the end of February, we never even thought about it. From then on, I never heard anyone complain about the name again."

But the disagreement over the name was an early lesson in the art of compromise, which would prove valuable for other decisions further down the line. Gráinne had agreed with Orla that it was the best name. Orla recalled:

> "In the end Ailbhe agreed, but it was difficult. It was important in terms of how we worked something out, and in the end Gráinne and I said to Ailbhe, 'you're out-voted here.' I remember saying 'if you're going to constantly undermine this all the way through it's going to be really difficult'. But Ailbhe said, 'No of course I'm not. Once the decision is made I'm behind it and I'll go out there and bat for it.' And that is exactly what she did. After that it was something the three of us did where, if we disagreed between ourselves, we would be very clear on why we disagreed, discuss it and then make a decision on what we believed was best for the campaign, and we always had a united front."

Agreement had finally been reached on the three groups – ARC, the Coalition to Repeal the Eighth Amendment and NWCI – coming together for the referendum campaign in early February.

Then came the idea of establishing a TFY campaign platform. Gráinne and Orla felt the campaign needed to be bigger than the three organisations. As Orla explained:

> "We felt the three organisations almost needed to take a step back and let the campaign be this wider platform, because that's what the Together for Yes was about. We're all in this together, it's not about ARC, the Women's Council, the Coalition; it's about the wider civil society campaign – that's something bigger than us."

But as Ailbhe remembered it, the idea of organising a platform, rather than building on the Coalition, seemed like duplication:

> "The idea was that we would need to have a platform that organisations could join up to and say 'Yes I'm for this.' A number of Coalition members thought this was unnecessary and were annoyed about it. We had a very stormy, intense Coalition meeting and it was definitely an uncomfortable time. In the end we didn't pursue it further – there was enough to be done elsewhere. The Together for Yes Platform was eventually agreed and it did bring in more organisations under the Repeal banner."

For Orla the way it all ended as a broader group meant it was more accessible to people who were nervous about getting involved.

On the political front, the Cabinet agreed the wording of what would replace the Eighth Amendment in the event of a Yes vote. It gave its approval to a bill formally allowing for a referendum to be called. This would propose that the article in the Constitution that recognises the equal right to life of the mother and the unborn child be deleted in its entirety and that a new clause be inserted that made it clear that the Oireachtas may legislate to regulate termination of pregnancy.

A further hurdle around this time, the beginning of March 2018, was awaiting a Supreme Court decision on the rights of the unborn. The Government had been waiting for the ruling. It concerned a judgment that found widespread rights within the Constitution and could have put the referendum in doubt. However during a historic first sitting of the court in Limerick, it delivered a unanimous ruling that the unborn had no constitutional rights outside the Eighth Amendment.

As it happened, just a day later the Coalition to Repeal the Eighth Amendment had organised a march to coincide with International Women's Day, on 8 March, and it was agreed to hold it under the new Together for Yes umbrella. Sinéad Kennedy remembered organising that march and deciding on a theme around the 100th anniversary of votes for women and tying that in with votes for Repeal and making history. But she hadn't factored in the arrival of that significant weather event 'the Beast from the East' and the unusual amount of snow that fell:

"We were in a state because of it. I'd no posters up. I was arguing with the Gardaí who were being horrible about where we could march. Then the Abortion Rights Campaign stepped in and said 'What do you need? We all need this to be great.' They really got us out of a hole putting up posters and leaflets. We began to use what would become HQ as a place where people could take posters and leaflets. NWCI helped out with the social media and we all came together around this. It got everybody into the mood."

At least 10,000 people attended that evening march and the atmosphere was electric: it was clear that activists were all set, 'raring to go' and calling for a firm referendum date.

The Together for Yes name was used for the first time the next morning when Sinéad did an interview for RTE Radio One current affairs programme *Morning Ireland*. During it she spoke of "trusting women to take the right decisions in consultation with their doctor, sometimes with their families, and to access abortion care in Ireland in a supportive environment."

"Should there be any protections for the unborn in law?" she was asked by presenter Audrey Carville. "I don't think that makes for very good laws", responded Sinéad. "And if we look at the whole history of the abortion debate in Ireland, putting abstract constitutional rights for the foetus has just created huge amounts of problems and if we trust women to care for their foetuses during their pregnancy that is the best and most practical way to care for every member of our society", she replied.

But the interviewer continued to press the point – no protection in law then specifically for the unborn right up until the point of birth? "Yes, I think that seems to be a very reasonable proposal, again putting the trust where it belongs", said Sinéad.

Sinéad knew afterwards she had performed well for the majority of the interview but had struggled on that issue of rights for the unborn baby:

"I wasn't happy with that. Because I was basically saying yes, but you had to put it in a better way, and I didn't do that. We needed to think about how we would answer that properly, and about how to reassure people who think 'Oh well I don't want that. I don't think a foetus should have no rights at all.' So how do you express that without saying that it has no rights in the Constitution? That was a key question."

It was an early lesson for the messaging of the campaign.

The Cabinet agreed the wording of what would replace the Eighth Amendment in the event that a vote to repeal it was passed. Voters would be asked whether they wanted to remove it and replace it with wording that would allow politicians to draw up Irish abortion laws in the future. If people voted yes the law would remain the Protection of Life During Pregnancy Act 2013 until any new legislation was passed. What the Government proposed allowed for access to terminations in certain circumstances. The 'general scheme' of a bill, which is its outline, and would become the

'Heads of a Bill', was produced to be debated by the Dáil, Seanad and Committee. Then if passed, the legislation would be accompanied by Medical Council guidelines.

That general scheme contained 22 headings – a number of them contentious, foremost the section relating to access to terminations within the first twelve weeks of pregnancy. There was also the circumstances in which abortion would be lawful between the twelfth and twenty-fourth week of pregnancy, as well as termination where there was a risk to the life or serious harm to the health of the mother in an emergency situation, which those opposed said would allow for abortions up to full term.

Then there was the section referring to terminations being made available in the cases of fatal foetal abnormalities. Those opposed claimed this could lead to abortions when a foetus is diagnosed with a non-fatal abnormality such as Down syndrome.

That same week the supporters of the Rally for Life, organised by the Life Institute, took to the streets, with numbers estimated at tens of thousands, calling for retention of the Eighth Amendment. Towards the end of March TDs voted by 97 to 27 to allow a referendum on abortion to go ahead.

Ailbhe remembered this period as a time of uncertainty and high anxiety, waiting for the different steps that needed to be taken by Government with much debate about what would follow if Repeal was successful. "There were ongoing discussions about the nature of the legislation following on from the recommendations of the Oireachtas Committee, because not everything was necessarily at all clear."

The general nervousness had been made worse by Tánaiste and Minister for Foreign Affairs Simon Coveney rocking Cabinet cohesion by saying in January he was in favour of Repeal but felt unable to support access to terminations up to twelve weeks. Fine Gael had a vote of conscience on this matter, as did Fianna Fáil, which meant he was free to vote in accordance with his own view. Senior ministers were bound to reach an official Cabinet position on the issue, but could campaign on either side of the argument during the campaign.

The Tánaiste would subsequently change his position and say he now backed the twelve-week proposal. However that decision was conditional on a number of additional safeguards being put in place. He sought the introduction of a 72-hour waiting period for women seeking an abortion, prohibition on late-term abortions and permitting access to abortion pills up to twelve weeks of gestation.

But his vacillating allowed the anti-abortion campaign to claim that politicians could not be trusted on this issue – a seemingly potent charge in an age when anti-political feeling was high. Mr Coveney would also call for a two-thirds majority lock if there were to be any further changes on abortion laws. This proposal was regarded as simply bizarre given that those with even a passing familiarity of constitutional law knew that such a thing was not possible. This understanding was subsequently confirmed by the Attorney General. Even more bizarrely, the Cabinet agreed that abortion law would go through a process 'above and beyond' what would normally be undertaken with legislation. At the time nobody knew exactly what this meant. The second most senior Cabinet member coming out in this way certainly caused huge uncertainty and hampered momentum. It had also given rise to concerns about the legislation on the availability of abortion up to twelve weeks subsequently passing in the Dáil.

But at long last, in mid-March the date for the referendum was announced. The vote would happen on Friday, 25 May 2018. Making the announcement, Minister for Health Simon Harris said it was time for the general electorate to have their say on the Eighth Amendment. A total of 3.2 million people would be eligible to vote, although no one under the age of 50 had previously had an opportunity to vote on the substantive issue. He predicted a close campaign, saying many people were just beginning to think about these deeply personal issues. It was to be a long eight-week campaign. Finally it was game on.

9

Together for Yes:
A United Front

~~~~~~~~~~~~~~~~~~~~~~~~~~~~~~~~~~~~~

There was a real buzz in the Pillar Room of the Rotunda Hospital. People seemed hardly able to believe the official launch of the Together for Yes national referendum campaign to remove the Eighth Amendment from the Constitution had finally arrived.

It hadn't been without incident though. The day before the Rotunda Hospital had distanced itself from the launch, saying it did not support any political organisation or agenda. This followed the Pro Life Campaign describing as "crass and insensitive" the decision of the group to launch its campaign in the grounds of the maternity hospital. It had also been difficult to find an MC for the launch because at that point prominent people were reluctant to align themselves with Together for Yes. The co-directors were very appreciative of author and journalist Martina Devlin for coming on board so willingly.

That morning there was standing room only. It was 22 March and there was a real sense of possibility in the air. There was cheering and hollering, and something not normally associated with abortion – joy. There were even standing ovations. Attendees included the Minister for Health, Simon Harris, indicating the backing of 'official' Ireland for the cause. The minister sat in the audience, as did the other politicians present. Together for Yes was presented as a national civil society campaign made up of over 70 organisations, groups and communities.

Groups such as the Rape Crisis Network Ireland, Women's Aid, the Irish Family Planning Association, the Union of Students in Ireland and the Well Woman Centre were all present for the launch. Those on stage sat under a large banner reading "Sometimes a private matter needs public support". A very deliberate picture was painted at this launch, to send the message this was an issue that went beyond reproductive rights, that had an impact on wider society, and, most importantly, that people cared about and wanted to see changed.

Everyone had been nervous in advance, worried about how things would go. Ailbhe, Gráinne and Orla were on stage and all spoke. The keynote address was delivered by former Supreme Court Judge Catherine McGuinness, who spoke about the impact of the constitutional amendment on the lives of women in Ireland and the doctors who cared for them. "I opposed the amendment in 1983 and I am a determined supporter of the Yes campaign this time round", she said. The lessons of the focus group research were applied. Dr Peter Boylan, chair of the Institute of Obstetricians and Gynaecologists, had a central role, as did Gaye and Gerry Edwards. The couple spoke very movingly of how they had been forced to travel to Belfast during their first pregnancy after being told their baby had a fatal foetal abnormality. "As a young man growing up

I never thought abortion would affect me, but it has. It affects us all", said Gerry. Ailbhe spoke of the central messages of the campaign: the three Cs of care, compassion and change.

It had been a big challenge to ensure that those speaking on behalf of the campaign were able to articulate support for abortion in the context of women's healthcare, calling it 'abortion care', avoiding absolutist or dogmatic statements about the importance of choice, but rather explaining why it was important for a woman to be able to make decisions about her own body. The campaign would begin as it meant to go on. The emphasis was on the need to talk with people, not to hector or lecture or shout, but to listen and respond conversationally. A consistently rational, calm tone, especially on social media, was used.

From the outside it all appeared to go off seamlessly but preparations had been frantic. A guide to the campaign structure and how internal communications would operate had been drawn up, following the earlier strategy sessions with Aoife Dermody, an expert in strategic development. A grid on which the entire campaign would operate showed the co-directors at the top, then the executive: Ailbhe; Sinéad Kennedy, secretary of the Coalition to Repeal the Eighth Amendment; Gráinne; Sarah Monaghan of the Abortion Rights Campaign; Orla; Silke Paasche, head of communications and membership at NWCI; and Niall Behan and Maeve Taylor from the Irish Family Planning Association. Then came the campaign manager, Deirdre Duffy. It set out a structure with separate work groups including communications; fundraising resources; political; mobilisation; evidence, data and risk; campaign supports involving governance, compliance and finance; volunteer coordinator; merchandise and shop; and administration.

The upper levels of the campaign would be "slim and hierarchical" to facilitate quick decision-making. It was agreed that decisions would be made by the executive, and signed off by the three co-directors. Failing consensus then a majority may decide. If guidance was needed it could be taken back to the executive, and all else failing a facilitator could be brought in. That document also stated how the co-directors would trust one another to have each other's backs and the interests of the campaign at heart, as well as working together in good faith, stick to agreements made, use confidential space to clarify any areas of disagreement and have a unified front for the rest of the campaign, and finally to "be loyal to one another."

The strategic advisory group was made up of commentator and barrister the late Noel Whelan; barrister Peter Ward; perinatal psychiatrist Veronica O'Keane and Dr Mark Murphy, who were both from Doctors for Choice; Adam May from Language; communications strategists Nikki Gallagher and Ronan Farren; social justice activist and co-founder of the Marriage Equality Campaign Denise Charlton; barrister Gráinne Gilmore; Labour senator and long-time pro-choice campaigner Ivana Bacik; and digital and social media expert Peter Tanham, plus the three co-directors.

So much had already been agreed and Orla, Ailbhe and Gráinne had been working together for a few months at that stage. But for everyone else it was a new experience and each of the three groups had a different organisational culture. Orla explained:

"In terms of finding the campaign manager it's difficult to find people who've got the sort of experience in terms of referendum campaigns and are available for that short period. We decided we would recruit two paid staff – campaign manager and communications manager. But it quickly became very clear in the comms area we needed more people than we had. In hindsight with the fundraising that was achieved we could have hired more comms staff from the beginning; however we had to start from the expectation of having a limited, small budget. We relied heavily on the goodwill of people to support and work on the campaign."

As soon as ARC came on board, Gráinne began work on a project plan and timeline for the campaign. She recalled pulling apart the book written on the marriage equality campaign, *Ireland Says Yes*, to examine their modus operandi. "Our governance and finance officer, Suzanne Handley, faced all sorts of delays getting the company set up", she recalls. Bank accounts were a "nightmare" to open. Cash flow remained a real issue for the first month. "Even though there were people saying 'let me help', 'let me give you ten grand', we had to say 'I'm sorry I just can't take it because of SIPO' [Standards in Public Office Commission]", said Gráinne. Similarly, ARC had plenty of funds but it could not donate them to Together for Yes.

As far as Ailbhe is concerned, all the hindsight in the world doesn't count for much given the particular situation they were in:

"We didn't have the opposition's war chest. They had stock-piled that war chest over years. It would have been very useful if we could have used funding from the Coalition in the start-up phase, but because of tough regulation of political campaigns in Ireland we could not do that. We simply could not use any money that we had received from outside Ireland."

An internal launch or 'campaign organising day' had been held two weeks before that official launch in the Rotunda. It involved various groups and activists, including those who had travelled from around the country – people who had been part of the fight to introduce abortion to Ireland for years. Held in the Teacher's Club in Dublin, after an introductory session presenting the overall campaign structure, those assembled were shown leaflets and branding and the Together for Yes logo. It was not all smooth sailing that day. A number of those at the meeting felt they had not been included in any of the decision-making processes, and that too much of what they were seeing had been influenced by research and focus groups. "That was again challenging", said Sarah Monaghan of ARC. "There were a lot of opinions in the room and a lot of people probably upset or disgruntled to say the least that they weren't at that top table, or that they hadn't been involved in different ways."

Gráinne, Ailbhe and Orla spoke and explained they would be the three co-directors for the campaign. Orla remembered the tensions, particularly around some of the messaging, which was presented by Adam May. For Gráinne:

" ... it was really the critical time of us saying 'we're putting all this to you, we hope you believe as we do that this is the way to win the referendum campaign.' It was having a real conversation about shifting into a different space from campaigning for abortion, to winning a referendum and mobilising the necessary over one million people to vote for repealing the Eighth. In the conversations that happened there was a really strong sense in the room of what's at stake here – we really have to win this because if we don't, when will we have this referendum again? We asked people to put their own groups aside for the next three months and form united Together for Yes groups. It was a really important meeting for all of us and built the ownership needed to make the campaign work effectively."

Incredibly, none of the information presented that night leaked ahead of the actual launch. The three co-directors explained how Together for Yes would be a national civil society campaign and bigger than the three organisations who established it. But a number of people felt that was needlessly encroaching on the territory of the Coalition to Repeal the Eighth, which had been established for the purpose of groups joining together and building into a bigger force. In time an understanding would grow that a Together for Yes civil society platform would provide an opportunity for organisations to identify and support abortion rights that had not done so to date.

In early March, barrister Deirdre Duffy was appointed as campaign manager, with former Labour Party official Amy Rose Harte as communications manager. Suzanne Handley was head of governance, compliance and finance. The communications team was Amy Rose; Silke Paasche, head of communicationss in NWCI; Denise Sammon, who worked in communications in London but returned home for the campaign; and Yvonne Judge, former RTE producer, who runs her own communications company. Yvonne set up the all-important 'Story Lab', where she gathered personal stories of abortion, key to the persuasion of voters. Sarah Clarkin, communications officer with NWCI, led the social media team, which succeeded in being one of the most impactful social media campaigns to date in Ireland.

Deirdre Duffy remembers going into the very large building on Lower Mount Street, which was to be the headquarters of the campaign, to find "nothing there". ARC had anticipated the need for a large referendum HQ premises the previous year and had been working with Denise Walker of the GMB Union to organise rental of their training college. The first job was to get desks, chairs and computers. Deirdre would later describe herself as taking over the management of a campaign with three organisations with four cultures, theirs and her own. She had worked previously as deputy director of the Irish Council for Civil Liberties and had a close relationship with the Coalition. She knew Ailbhe and Sinéad Kennedy well, and said she had a great respect for Orla and NWCI. Gráinne and Deirdre had built a relationship working on Standards in Public Office Commission (SIPO) regulations in previous years and Deirdre had briefed the pre-referendum ARC EGM on legal issues. Having closely observed the progress of the various pro-choice groups over the previous years, Deirdre really believed in Ailbhe's ability to lead and be the glue to hold it all together:

> "My own view at that time, and I think probably correct in hindsight as well, was that eventually Ailbhe and Sinéad Kennedy were really holding the [political] Left, and that that's where we had failed in the past. This was going to fragment if somebody like Ailbhe didn't hold it together and she was kind of the only person who could ever do it."

During the early stages there would have been an element of managing the politics at the table, said Deirdre:

> "But of course in the early days as well you have to listen and talk to a lot of people who have a lot of opinions on what should be happening and what shouldn't be happening. I don't mind that, that's fine, but there comes to a point then when you're saturated, and you just have to make a decision."

Amy Rose said it would have been odd not to have had natural tensions but mostly people got on with the business of the campaign:

"I think it was a strength of the co-directors that they had a similar, collaborative approach to negotiating, to ironing out issues. The passion was across the board from every corner. And I think that's what brought people together. There was a real sense of realism when we started. To be fair, people came on board with opinions and histories. There was a sense of reality and pragmatism about what needed to be done. And I did find that a lot of those foot soldiers, whether in ARC or the Coalition or NWCI, were able to put their different opinions aside and to take direction from leadership."

Given her experience of various campaigns over the years, Ailbhe said that once you get into campaign mode:

"You are so busy with the nuts and bolts of everyday business that you don't talk about what you might think of as wider ideological differences or problems, you really don't. You're just getting on with it."

Deirdre said she worked at getting everything moving:

"My job then was to just move, move, move, and keep moving around making decisions and getting the machine cranked up and going forward .... It would be untrue of me to say that in the early days I wasn't also fearful. I think I was most fearful about the pace."

Deirdre remembered on her first day meeting Amy Rose, with whom she would go on to form a close working relationship. They were, she said, an "unlikely duo". She was a dyed-in-the-wool pro-choice activist who had never run a political campaign, while Amy Rose was unfamiliar with activism but very familiar with politics, particularly from a rural perspective with her grandfather Paddy Harte having represented Donegal as a TD for decades and her father, Jimmy Harte, as a Senator. She had worked as a parliamentary assistant in Leinster House before moving to the Labour Party press office.

> "Amy Rose really didn't know abortion politics at all and would say that herself. So for the first few weeks we would be asking the stupid questions. But in many ways that really helped us because she had that lens for the moveable middle, for middle Ireland, that is very difficult for somebody like me to always have. I met her the first day in the hall of the HQ building with Silke Paasche from NWCI. We just got on and we had a very good working relationship that survived through everything. And I think we had one time of maybe cross words and that was it, although we didn't always agree either."

Deirdre said she "probably drove them all demented in the early stages" talking to everyone working on the campaign about operating off the same system, how they were organising themselves, what they had written down, how they were storing things and everyone working off Google Drive:

> "The mechanics of campaigning, even though some people would resist them, actually are what allow the dynamics to really take off because it's simple and because nobody is going around saying: 'where's that photograph that we took yesterday' because they knew exactly where it is."

For Deirdre one of the great successes of the campaign was how people managed to put aside any reservations they might have had because they realised there was a shared value and everyone was headed in the same direction:

> "I think it was one of the most impressive things ... you know even in HQ where I was obviously most of the time we'd hundreds of people coming in and out. It was always energy; it was always

> positive. There was plenty of giving out, but people just got on with it."

NWCI receives core funding from the State and was therefore in a different position to the Coalition and ARC regarding the use of funding and staff to work on the campaign. Four staff members – Silke Paasche; Sarah Clarkin; Laura Harmon, head of mobilisation team; and Eilís Ní Chaithnía, joint head of platform – moved to HQ with Orla for the campaign. Staff worked part-time on the campaign and part-time with NWCI. Salaries were paid with non-State funding for the period worked on the campaign. Any additional hours worked by staff were on a voluntary basis and no overtime was accumulated. NWCI still had to deliver on a full programme of work. While it was difficult, Orla remains cognisant of the brilliant commitment of the NWCI team, who all went the extra mile that year as they were so passionate about winning the referendum and doing everything to achieve it.

They also had to fundraise to pay the salaries of those who worked on the campaign in HQ, including Orla. "It was a huge struggle. We were all doing time sheets as part of our SIPO and State compliance. But trying to fundraise at the same time as the Together for Yes fundraising was a complete waste of time. We ended up using NWCI reserves and we will have to build them up again in the coming years."

Setting up a campaign structure primarily based on volunteers had huge challenges, and trying to do so with no money made that all the more so. Mary Coogan, a member of ARC, had a background in volunteer management. She was able to take time off work to look after volunteer coordination for the campaign. Finding volunteers was not a problem. In fact the opposite was the case, and ultimately there were a total of 330 of them in HQ. But many of those offering to volunteer had full-time jobs. Others took time off closer to polling day.

Mary matched what needed to be worked on – such as the online shop or the pop-up shops or admin tasks in HQ which required specific skills – to the number of hours people had available and whether they could work during the day or not. Often she would redirect people to their home canvassing groups, asking them to get out on the doorsteps. At one stage later in the campaign Mary had to make the decision to close down the section of the website where volunteers signed up, after it peaked at 1,000:

> "I couldn't stay on top of the level of interest. People just appeared. It was quite overwhelming. Everything is so fast-paced and it's taking the time to step back and say 'Okay I need actually five people to do this.' It's really hard because everything is going all of the time. But really it was just like this giant machine that just worked."

On the age profile of the volunteers, Mary said it was mostly younger women, mid-20s, and a "smattering of men".

The average campaign day started at 7 a.m. for the core team, with a communications call at 7.30 involving Ailbhe, Gráinne, Orla, Sarah Monaghan, Deirdre and Amy Rose, to discuss media coverage and responses that might be needed, as well as events later that day. HQ was usually full by 9.30 a.m., often with around 60 people, but with lots of people coming and going throughout the day. Different offices looked after areas such as digital marketing, social media, fundraising, advertising, merchandise, and mobilisation. A large room at the front housed merchandise and the Together for Yes and ARC online shops, where the original ARC shop volunteer crew ran a full-time assembly line staffed by hundreds of volunteers working in shifts.

Hundreds of fundraising events took place all over the country during that period and it was a big logistical operation to organise and send volunteers to sell merchandise. At the beginning of May there was a Register to Vote campaign. Around the same time U2 tweeted their support for a Yes vote.

As well as getting the nuts and bolts of the campaign up and running, there were still live issues that needed to be addressed. There was a lot of controversy around the Government's proposals, particularly the delay period of 72 hours for women wishing to have an abortion, disabilities, and testing for Down syndrome, all of which the campaign had to deal with, as well as stressing that the only way to provide for cases of fatal foetal abnormality was to allow for abortion up to later stages of pregnancy. During the referendum, and since then, there remained significant anger from some quarters that twelve weeks had been 'accepted' as the cut-off point for abortion on request. But at that early point in the campaign, even that timescale proved very difficult for some people who felt it was actually a step too far and they weren't sure if they could bring themselves to vote for it. As Ailbhe recalled:

> "I remember one of our strategy meetings where Mark Garrett [former adviser to former Labour party leader Eamon Gilmore, who volunteered on the campaign] was saying the twelve weeks was actually a kind of poisoned chalice. You know we needed it desperately and we were very pleased, but it was hugely problematic in the first month of the campaign. The other side was out there with posters showing a foetus, which offended many parents who were trying to deal with their children saying on the way to school or outside the shopping centre: 'What is that Mammy?' Those posters, by the way, were the other side's first mistake. They should have taken those down immediately."

But the campaign was not without its humorous moments, according to Ailbhe:

> "The big issue was around when the clock started ticking for the twelve weeks. In fact, you start counting from the first day of your last menstrual period (LMP). There was a long discussion about LMPs at one particular meeting, with a lot of back and forth, and with a number of men getting quite red in the face. At the end of the discussion I said that we should have recorded it!"

On the No side there were two main separate groups involved in the campaign: Save the 8th, which involved the Life Institute, Youth Defence and 140 local groups; and Love Both, which originated in the Pro Life Campaign. The Iona Institute, which describes itself as an inter-denominational group that believes children, once conceived, have a right to be born, also had a very active and often controversial role.

At one point the Love Both campaign issued a statement saying it had "no connection whatsoever" with an anti-abortion group calling itself the Irish Centre for Bio-Ethical Reform (ICBR), and did not condone their actions. That group, using a deliberate strategy of shock tactics, displayed extreme imagery, with large bloody photographs, which it claimed were dismembered foetuses, outside Dublin's three maternity hospitals.

This led to some of the most marvellously gleeful and appreciated moments in the campaign. A group called Radical Queers Resist took to arriving at these ICBR protests and used white sheets, pride flags and rainbow flags to cover up the offensive images from the public, most particularly women and their partners going to and from the maternity hospitals.

At the beginning of her stint Deirdre Duffy, who worked for 86 days on the campaign, had a chat with barrister and commentator Noel Whelan, a member of the strategic advisory group. "I liked his style. You'd talk for a few minutes and you'd get three really good things out of him. He's very insightful and he's not sitting in front of you for an hour talking about himself."

On the basis of the advice from Noel, who had been a key figure in the marriage equality campaign, each morning Deirdre would check in with four different campaign 'screens' to assess progress – canvas returns, what was coming in on the ground; what had turned up on the media monitoring in terms of coverage; opinion polls; and listening to what had been said by advisers:

> "In the morning I would check the media monitoring, I'd check the canvassing returns and every evening you'd think through what was coming. You're trying to see around corners."

Those canvas returns formed a key part of the campaign. They were input on a newly developed software package which had been specially designed for the campaign. The digital team set about coming up with a canvas returns system, involving technical solutions for collecting and analysing canvas data, as well as trying to capture some of the sentiment being heard on the doorsteps. The team of around twenty people was led by Peter Tanham.

The digital team brainstormed on what would be the best canvassing system to put in place with Annie Hoey, the Coalition's regional officer and a former head of the Union of Students in Ireland, who was part of the mobilisation team which was managing local groups around the country. They wanted to devise a plan that maximised the time spent canvassing. This meant looking at the 'run rate', which was how many houses could be visited in one canvas, and how many canvasses it would take to get an entire constituency done. Initially there was a canvas return sheet with a scale of 5 to 1, a 1 being a response that was hostile and a definite No and a 5 being a strong 'I'm a Yes vote and I'll definitely vote on the day.' The difficulty, they soon realised, was the subjectivity in judging people's response, with canvassers trying to work out what was a 3 or a 4. So after discussion the sheet was changed to a simpler Yes/No/Maybe or 'Didn't want to engage.' The tech team then set up a logging system that included a comment section so particular issues coming up could be flagged.

It took a while to get it right given that in one night there could be hundreds of canvas groups covering a few thousand homes. The team built a user-friendly interface which gave them headline figures – the number of Yeses, the number of Nos, the number of Maybes and some form of street name. Deirdre Duffy had a policy document on data protection done up and for GDPR reasons they didn't go any further than that with the information. The information gathered gave the ability to deep-dive on a constituency level, especially as time went on and the sample size got bigger. By the end of the campaign it would be estimated that 19,000 canvassers had worked with 110 local Together for Yes groups.

Each night team leads around the country, at the conclusion of a canvas, or a local digital person, would feed the details into the system so the information was there the next morning for the team coming into HQ. For the final few weeks the sample size was around 6,000 data points, in other words 6,000 individual houses canvassed. Comments included in the canvas reports would be passed on to Laura Harmon, who oversaw the mobilisation team. The system, which had been built up with great commitment and expertise by the team of volunteers, caused considerable interest and intrigue outside of the campaign. The information it fed back meant the campaign could remain confident they were on the right course.

When Deirdre Duffy sat at her desk the office walls surrounding her were covered with "campaign stuff" stuck up there. She said a big part of her job was having a strong relationship with key team members and picking up information from them, including possible nuggets from those canvas returns, and acting on it when necessary:

> "Someone might pop into me and say we're getting interesting returns coming back from Limerick or Donegal or wherever, or there's an interesting trend here about abortion pills, for example. About a month out it was about abortion pills becoming the new contraception, which was being picked up as part of the No side's messaging. Obviously the No camp had gone to the doors and that was their message. So that was coming up in very particular pockets. I remember it was Limerick initially. So we could tackle that kind of trend by asking, maybe, Dr Mark Murphy of Doctors for Choice to go on local radio in Limerick and counter that."

Getting the message out about the reality of abortion pills in Ireland was really important. The UK published statistics on women from Ireland accessing abortion in their clinics. However in reality abortion pill use was underground, invisible and illegal. Gráinne drew on connections made through lobbying work with the international charity Women Help Women to convince that organisation to release their Irish data:

> "They had reservations, and we were working at an incredible pace; plans changed by the hour. Meanwhile, the Irish media

kept reporting abortion pills as dangerous, which horrified them as they supply prescription grade medication and only when appropriate. They were really worried about how the media coverage would affect the women in touch with them. I was drawing on every ounce of friendship and trust that I had and they came through for us. They released regional and national figures that showed 878 women in Ireland used their service in 2017, and the figures continued to rise. In the first three months of 2018, 323 women ordered pills online, a 90 per cent increase on the same period in 2017. We were bringing an Irish reality out of the shadows."

Throughout the campaign, Together for Yes held regular press conferences where position papers were launched on carefully chosen topics. These explained complex or controversial issues to people through the media, and also worked to establish the credibility of the campaign. Deirdre said it was also a case of going out and "owning our own Achilles' heels". There were then, of course, other issues raised throughout the campaign by the No side, such as claiming the grounds of mental health would be abused by women to seek a termination or the Save the 8th billboard campaign featuring a little boy that had the message: "In Britain 90% of babies with Down's Syndrome are aborted. Save Lives. Save the 8th."

For years the vast majority of doctors had been afraid to speak out on abortion for fear of repercussion – be it legally or on their career. But the dam broke during the campaign and Together for Yes definitely facilitated that. Amy Rose remembered obstetricians being invited to HQ to film videos of support. Those who took up the invitation included obstetrician Dr Maeve Eogan, medical director of the Sexual Assault Treatment Unit at the Rotunda Hospital, whom Amy Rose saw as a "critical medical voice"; Professor Mary Higgins, obstetrician at the National Maternity Hospital, who would also speak at the launch of the Fine Gael campaign for a Yes vote; Professor Louise Kenny, previously of Cork University Maternity Hospital and Pro-Vice-Chancellor, Health and Life Sciences at the

University of Liverpool; and Dr Jennifer Donnelly, obstetrician at the Rotunda Hospital. "The way in which that group of doctors mobilised was incredible", said Amy Rose.

The first press conference, on 5 April, seven weeks from voting day, outlined just why abortion should be made lawful up to twelve weeks and how, on the issue of rape, the removal of the Eighth Amendment would allow for the provision of compassionate, non-judgemental care to women and girls. At the top table were Orla, Dr Maeve Eogan, and Niamh Ní Dhomhnaill, who spoke of her personal experience of rape.

Niamh told the journalists the Eighth Amendment was a trauma-inducing law removing bodily control from any pregnant woman. Free, safe and legal abortion was crucial for those who found themselves pregnant as a result of rape. Dr Maeve Eogan said the twelve-week gestational limit was sufficiently long for victims of sexual violence to realise they are pregnant and for them to seek terminations at that time. Margaret Martin, then director of Women's Aid, also spoke.

The next press conference happened, Deirdre Duffy remembered, at "one of our most dangerous moments" and concerned fatal foetal abnormalities. The No side had begun to shift the debate slightly in terms of saying abortion should be available in such situations, but in no way as broadly as was being proposed. "It was a clever tactic from them and they should have done it earlier …. We needed to go out first thing on that Monday morning and shut it down because otherwise it would have got legs and the media would have picked it up."

That press conference was chaired by Ailbhe and fronted by senior counsel Peter Ward, who had campaigned in 1983 against the insertion of the Eighth Amendment in the Constitution, barrister Gráinne Gilmore, and Liam Herrick, executive director of the Irish Council for Civil Liberties.

Towards the end of that same week another press conference was held with Dr Jennifer Donnelly and bereavement midwife Jane Dalrymple, both from the Rotunda Hospital. Dr Donnelly told the media:

"The Eighth Amendment prevents me from providing complete pregnancy care to women when they are at their most vulnerable. It prevents me from being there for women when they deliver and it limits me from offering them further investigations such as post-mortems which may help guide their care in future pregnancies."

Dr Siobhán Donohue, national chair of the Terminations for Medical Reasons (TMFR) group, told her own story:

"I was one of Jane's [Dalrymple] patients in 2011. During my third pregnancy my baby was diagnosed with anencephaly. Myself and my husband were devastated. Our world was turned upside down. We will always remember the compassionate care we received from Jane and her colleagues before we travelled, but their hands were tied. They could not offer us the care we needed because of the Eighth amendment."

She travelled to the Liverpool Women's Hospital where she was told there was a room nicknamed 'the Shamrock Suite' as so many Irish women had been in it.

A big campaign moment was the National Doctors Together for Yes Summit in Dublin, which involved medics from all over the country gathering in Dublin. Over 1,000 doctors (it would rise to 1,500 before polling day), from every county, had signed a public declaration of their support for Repeal. As Amy Rose explained:

"The women were the heroes of the campaign and the doctors were able to bring voters into the ward and paint these pictures of their hands being tied by the Constitution when trying to treat women. ... The doctors were able to appeal in terms of medical facts and what the Irish electorate wanted to hear, which was logic. They didn't want bluster. They didn't want stories about process. There was a huge potential for us on a daily basis to be dragged into process stories about funding or about posters or whatever. And yes we had to answer those questions, but our strategy was to focus on the issues and to win people over on the basis of logic. The doctors were an extraordinary force in the extent to which they moved from fronting some press conferences to actually mobilising en masse and actively campaigning. We emphasised and put the message repeatedly to the Irish people that abortion was already a reality in Ireland. We did it by creating moments and managing the news cycle. We were constantly repeating that message, as well as that of abortion pills, which was enormous."

10

A Nationwide Campaign and the Irish Yes

Donegal is well-known for being a conservative county when it comes to voting on social issues. In general Cathie Shiels found the experience of canvassing for the referendum positive; there were obviously a lot of people who were anti-abortion but they weren't rude about it. However there is one man she canvassed for a Yes vote who does stand out in her memory:

> "He followed me out onto the street calling me a murderer. I had a fight-or-flight response, but I thought if I keep running down

> the street he will follow me. So I turned and I said to him, 'have you lost the run of yourself?'"

The approach worked and the man left her alone. Cathie had had an abortion when she was nineteen and living in Scotland. She returned to Ireland and had not thought about it for a while until she saw those 2012 Youth Defence billboard ads, which had served to incense so many women and driven them to become active in the Repeal movement. She was involved, alongside activist Sinéad Redmond, in setting up the Facebook page 'Unlike Youth Defence I trust women to decide their lives for themselves'.

Cathie joined ARC, and she helped to set up groups all over the country, doing workshops on how to talk to people about abortion. "We had a list of 100 different questions so we would use role-playing, asking the question, giving the response, and then reading the suggested response, then adding suggestions to it."

Cathie works as a civil servant at clerical officer grade – a rank, she explained, where she is allowed to be politically active, but she could not be promoted while doing so. For the campaign she took off the last two weeks of April and the first two of May and returned to her home county, where she had been organising since August 2017. There had been a pro-choice group there previously but it had fallen away. She revived it and by November 2017 had a strong core group of ten people.

Cathie is originally from Carndonagh in Inishowen. On a week-night during the campaign there would usually have been four people out canvassing, but it could have been as low as two or as high as six. "We managed to get all of the housing estates done, but there were lots of houses in the country along the road, or half a mile in from the road, that we wouldn't have made." They canvassed every night, and ran a stall on a Saturday. Lots of people would take lifts home from Dublin at the weekend for a super canvas on a Saturday.

There were a lot of Yeses on the doorsteps, but some nights, in particular areas, there would be very firm and definite Nos:

"One day I knocked on a door without first seeing the Sacred Heart hanging there, with about one hundred rosary beads hanging off it. The woman answered the door and said 'we don't believe in that here.' But she wasn't hateful or anything."

All of the local groups had set up their own internal structures and were communicating through a range of local WhatsApp and Facebook groups. Laura Harmon, head of mobilisation team, established a national WhatsApp networking group for groups to share ideas, photos, etc. WhatsApp meant there was really good communications between the groups around the country, with photos being shared of things like a coffee morning or a stall. As Cathie recalled:

"There is a bit of notoriety about Donegal and people associate it with a contrarian vote, so lots of people would get in touch when they would see our photos and say, 'well if you're managing it there in Donegal we have no excuse not to get moving.' I knew it was probably going to be a No in Donegal. I know Donegal is conservative. While the levels of canvassing had been even enough across the Yes and No sides, there were nights when it wasn't at all. People were sweet afterwards saying 'well the county voted yes', but it didn't; we were about 2,000 short."

Mary Coogan, who worked as volunteer coordinator in HQ, also canvassed in Dublin. Working with other ARC members in early 2018, she put together canvassing training and a canvassing guide with typical questions:

"My experience in my own constituency in Dublin in the Crumlin/Rialto area, for example, was that the issue of disability, for instance, was seldom brought up. The most common block, or the thing that people seem to stick on, was twelve weeks on request. When you talked through the rationale people generally kind of understood it. I was expecting a certain amount of 'you're all murderers; you're all baby killers.' I wasn't expecting the attitudes towards women that were coming from people who probably were going to vote yes, and who were middle of the road. In a lot of ways they just had this really dismissive attitude towards women and towards women's lives and health, and that old line that abortion would be used as contraception.

I remember one time when somebody said that and I asked 'who are these women who you think are going to have fifteen abortions? Is it me?' and they said, 'No, no, not you.' So I said, 'Who are these mythical women?' There was also the 'well if you've made your bed lie on it' kind of attitude. But there was no single across-the-board or shared response from certain age profiles or genders, which surprised me a bit. I met so many older people on the doors who were just so open you could tell they had really experienced, I guess, life at the sharp end around reproductive health. Older people who had gone on the journey, and in some cases were really grappling with their faith; where their conscience was telling them one thing, and their faith another. I definitely learned that when someone opens the door, and you look at them and you think they are going to say a certain thing, that in actuality you cannot predict their response. I never had any very negative experiences on the doorsteps, but I do know they were part and parcel of the campaign."

Sinéad Kennedy, the co-founder of the Coalition and a member of the Together for Yes executive, had gone on a number of Dublin canvasses and usually nine out of ten times it was a Yes. But when canvassing in rural areas she noticed that it wasn't that people were saying No; instead they wouldn't say anything:

"I suppose I was interpreting that as a polite No; in retrospect it was a polite 'Yes, but I don't want to talk about it.' So what we thought was maybe a No was an Irish Yes. We were quite confident about holding Dublin, but less so for the rest of the country and how much weight that would hold."

She remembers being on doorsteps and people revealing things like that they had had an abortion, or a woman on a doorstep in Tipperary who told her she had given up a child for adoption, and that she had never told her other children or her husband:

> "I got talking to her and she just said: 'I don't know. And this whole thing is just so hard.' A lot of older people would talk about how hard it was to be a woman in Ireland. I know there were times I was judgemental. I would see someone, maybe a very conservative-looking farmer, and I'd think, 'well he's a No.' And then he would say, 'I'm definitely a Yes.'"

Sinéad and Maeve Taylor of the Irish Family Planning Association had worked on a detailed Messaging Book – an almost 15,000-word document that was a cornerstone of the campaign – which aimed to answer any and every question relating to abortion. It gave key messages, as well as a series of questions and answers with key statistics, details on how to fundraise and canvas, and tips on communications strategies.

There were short and long versions of why to vote Yes, words to use and avoid when canvassing for a Yes vote, what the Eighth Amendment was, and why it needed to be repealed, how it had affected the lives and health of women. It had evidence from doctors.

Under the heading 'Words to Use' it advised canvassers to speak of 'personal decision', 'when medically necessary', 'never easy', 'regulated', 'doctor's care'. With words to avoid it was 'choice', 'on demand', 'without restriction/unrestricted', 'free', 'right to choose', 'on request' or 'bodily autonomy'.

A message at the beginning from the three co-directors, directed at advocates and canvassers, told them they were the most important ambassadors, and through them that members of the public would engage with Together for Yes. It urged them to treat the document confidentially and to manage access to it very carefully:

> "Over the next eight weeks, we will build a movement for care, compassion and change that will reach every home, village and

town across the country. We will canvas, fundraise, organise and mobilise. Most importantly we will talk, respectfully and inclusively, telling stories and explaining facts, we will bring people together from all backgrounds, life experiences and perspectives to work together towards one common goal."

Everyone, it said, is entitled to their view on abortion; it is a very personal issue. It gave detailed responses to the assertions most commonly put forward by the other side in arguing against abortion, such as 'floodgates' opening and the abortion rate increasing if the Eighth was repealed, and that it would lead to an increase in the terminations of Down syndrome pregnancies, that there would be abortion up to birth, that the Eighth had 'saved' 100,000 lives. No one, the Messaging Book explained, would be allowed to end a pregnancy on the grounds of foetal anomaly that would cause disability. Access to abortion would be safe and regulated through law and medical and ethical guidelines. There would be new measures to reduce the need for abortion through education and contraception. In answer to the question of why it is essential that women are able to request an abortion up to twelve weeks it stated, "The vast majority of women who have abortions do so before 12 weeks. All of the evidence shows that this is the key area of need."

Moving on to fundraising, the document also outlined how, as the national civil society campaign, Together for Yes intended to raise up to €500,000 for the referendum campaign but was entirely dependent on the generosity of the public to generate the funds. It gave examples of what different amounts could fund: for instance €1,000 would pay for four information evenings about the Eighth Amendment in different parts of rural Ireland; €500 would pay for 50 posters; €100 for a day's canvassing training; €50 for targeted ads on social media reaching 2,000 undecided voters; or €20 for 1,000 Yes information booklets delivered to homes around the country.

Together for Yes had registered with SIPO and according to its rules the limit for an individual's donation is €2,500. Organisations and groups based in Ireland were allowed to donate to the campaign but any organisation that wished to donate over €200 had to be registered with SIPO as a corporate donor. As well as that, any one organisation could only donate up to a maximum of €2,500. From abroad, only funds from Irish citizens were allowed.

Sinéad Kennedy said that very early on queries were raised on the posters put up by the Save the 8th campaign, such as "In England 1 in 5 babies are aborted" and the claim that 90 per cent of pregnant women in the UK who get a Down syndrome diagnosis will have an abortion. There was also the poster with a picture of a surprised-looking baby saying: "'I had No idea ...'" and the tagline: "They want to legalise abortion up to 6 months"; "6 months is horrific. Vote No" stated another. These posters led to the realisation that the sort of specific detail contained in the Messaging Book was necessary, not just with a straightforward, factual answer, but also to give context. Sinéad elaborated:

> "It wasn't as simple as saying 'No, they're wrong.' What Maeve Taylor and I spent a long time trying to figure out, obviously with input from lots of other people, was how do we answer these questions. What we wanted to create were answers that fitted in with the messages we were putting forward. Obviously Maeve, from working in the Irish Family Planning Association, had a lot of expertise in this whole area."

As a Together for Yes local group convenor, Richael Carroll was very familiar with that messaging. Once the referendum was announced she did a callout for people in Co. Mayo who wished to canvas. She organised a meeting and had twenty names and thought maybe half of those might turn up. But on the day everyone did and she was so pleased and surprised she immediately took a photo and sent it to the *Connaught Telegraph*.

Richael, who lives outside Kiltimagh, had never trained anyone but that day the twenty would-be canvassers were put through their paces with the Together for Yes messaging. The county was then divided into four areas with two representatives in each. Volunteers were also referred down from HQ. They would be sent to their own area so that in the end each region had up to twenty canvassers. Communication was conducted via WhatsApp. Each of the four areas had their own messaging group, and there was also an overall group which constantly gave updates on canvasses or live commentary on TV debates or news reports:

> "Even if you weren't watching a debate it was as if you were with all the comments. There was also a lot of venting and discussion and support and debriefing. Technology can be brilliant when it's doing good things."

Canvassing happened around four times a week, sometimes every night. There were street stalls. One of the most frightening experiences of the campaign happened at a street stall in Westport after which Richael made a report to An Garda Síochána. "It is not where people would have assumed it would have happened, given that Westport is really trendy and artsy, but that's a facade on top of a very conservative underbelly that runs very deep." She was at the stall with other women, some of whom had young children, including some asleep in buggies. A man began to shout at them and was recording the interaction:

> "He was shouting and pointing his finger and telling us we were murderers and baby killers .... I'm not really the kind to be afraid. I don't freeze in those situations. I go into Superwoman mode. I made myself as big as possible and came out from behind the table. I just made myself a barrier between him and the kids. I have to say, though, that this was an exceptional case, and there were only a few incidents like that. Some people would get incredibly upset when it would happen and I would just take them aside and give them a piece of chocolate, and they were usually fine. I know that some weren't expecting it even though it would come up in training and we had spoken about the worst thing that could happen."

Initially Richael was nervous about the canvassing, but ultimately found it to be fine:

"There was maybe one person per estate who was irate. At the start, around four weeks out, most people didn't know, or they were confused, or they were men who felt it was nothing to do with them or said they didn't know what the big deal was. We would ask: 'Are you married? Do you have sisters? Were you born from a woman?' We usually kept on script, but we deviated depending on who we were talking to, or what we were talking about."

Richael found that most of the older people they spoke to were "totally" on board. "The most frustrating people were my age, people in their thirties, who were staunch Nos. It would be a woman with a baby on her hip and another in the kitchen."

Canvassers kept note of all the responses and fed the information back to their 'numbers person', who passed it back to the digital team in Dublin. "It was always very positive really. There were very few places that we canvassed where the Nos outweighed the Yes. There was always more Yes than No", Richael recalled.

Kathy D'Arcy was the chair of the Cork Together for Yes group. Cork has a strong history of abortion activism and Kathy said people like Sandra McEvoy and Alan Gibson had been campaigning before her on the issue for decades and were members of the Coalition. She was part of the Rebels for Choice group that had been operating in more recent years and had become involved with ARC. In 2017 they became the official Cork branch of ARC. They also set about bringing together groups in Cork interested in Repeal, at one stage having 22 core groups, and linking into the Coalition.

That network, with its volunteer base, was easily able to switch into Cork Together for Yes. A key factor, she said, was that the group had a city centre office as a base – a former TV repair shop. After the campaign, for a short while, it was turned into a community space. Kathy worked to make sure the office was somewhere volunteers could come to chat or have a cup of tea or make badges or to have a discussion if they were upset. Volunteers worked there processing data from the canvas returns or doing graphic design. Kathy was passionate about taking a positive approach to the referendum, in using creativity, and in making sure that something would be found for anyone who wished to be involved. She put up a 'Positivity Wall' to which everyone could contribute using, amongst other materials, yellow stickies, crayons, markers and glitter. There were loads of pictures drawn by children. A yoga instructor gave classes. People could embroider cushions.

"These were all things that I brought because it's so important to take a positive approach and that was very much the Together for Yes approach all along. I cried when we took down that Positivity Wall, and I still have it all. If I ever live in a house big enough I'll put it back up. There was a young guy who used to come in and he wanted to do something to help but didn't want to engage with the public, which I understood. I just kept chatting to him and eventually it turns out he was an animator, and he made a beautiful animation about how to get to your polling station."

The video ended up being used nationally.

A big fan of creative activism, Kathy used to go out dressed as a superhero character – 'Repeal Woman' – to marches or street stalls and even once to Leinster House. There was even a 'Make Your Own Repeal Woman' stall over the years. "There are so many benefits to bringing creativity into activism. It turns anger into laughter and really brings people on board."

As the largest county in Ireland, Cork had a lot of canvassing ground to cover. There were around 17 regional groups and they organised training for canvassers, operating from the Together for Yes Messaging Book. Kathy said that volunteers, mainly young people in their twenties from all over the county, stepped up to lead these regional groups. Once trained up, they in turn would train the local volunteers. There were hundreds out each night. "They would drop everything every night and canvassed the entire county. It was an incredible network of training that started at the top and then spiralled down."

As far as Kathy was concerned the messaging was absolutely key:

"It was the messaging that worked. It was amazing. We saw the results in so many of the conversations we had started. It was because of the training we had received, and the attitude of positivity and openness to dialogue, and trying not to foster conflict. Many of the people we met at the door ended up changing to a more moderate position. You know, the other thing that happened was they actually then came out and voted Yes."

She said the experience of using that approach of discussion and listening and openness has taught her so much, even in her personal life:

"I went from being somebody who would have arguments with people, and use social media to give out. I had a realisation to do with that training, that actually you're not going to bring anyone with you by creating polarisation; if people witness you as an angry person shouting at another angry person they won't care what side you are on, they just want to get away .... But if they see normal, ordinary people being open ... saying they want to be compassionate, it's easier to get involved. That positivity has really changed me."

Coming into the campaign, ARC had a network of 36 ARC groups across the country with whom they had worked on language and branding. Some were more active, larger and more self-sufficient than others. All of the groups within ARC downed their ARC branding for the campaign and built alliances locally to establish local Together for Yes groups. New local groups popped up in the gaps, led by enthusiastic and energetic campaigners who set up campaigning and canvassing operations stretching the length and breadth of the country. Other grassroots networks did similar; Parents for Choice began as a Facebook group in 2014 which created an online space for parents to discuss abortion and developed into an active campaigning group with over 3,000 members. In advance of the referendum the group changed its name to 'Parents Together for Yes'.

Looking to HQ for support and resources, relationships didn't always run smoothly. One of the issues after the campaign that was raised was the interactions between these groups and HQ. Sometimes the groups felt they were not getting enough support from HQ and that the campaign was too centralised. Many felt it was easier to canvas in urban areas where Yes voters were perhaps more comfortable about showing their support or were less conservative, and that it was a tougher ask in more rural areas. Deirdre Duffy felt that some of these groups could have done afterwards with a bit of self-reflection about how they engaged with the women in HQ who were working so hard and for such long hours, the vast majority on a voluntary basis, and who in the end were just doing their best:

> "The mobilisation team suffered quite a lot of personal and professional haranguing, potentially maybe a little bit of abuse, from local groups who found it very difficult. I also realise we should have done more in terms of recognising that and supporting them."

Sarah Monaghan, who had been involved with establishing those local groups around the country over years, said while you expected to feel pressure from the other side what had been really difficult was internal criticism from stakeholder organisations on the Together for Yes platform:

> "It hurt more when it came from people you'd been working with for years. People were in the office working 18-hour days and doing their best. That was very hard for a lot of people to take. I suppose it was that thing that you probably get in any campaign with people forgetting that they were dealing with other people involved in the same struggle as them. Again we could maybe have done things slightly differently to try to alleviate that earlier, but we didn't have the resources to do so. So I don't want to sugarcoat it, but I do remember it all very fondly overall. I think most people do. But they were very difficult times and it was high stress."

Ultimately, 500,000 doors were knocked on all over the country. During the campaign the co-directors, Ailbhe, Gráinne and Orla, were always conscious of not wanting the campaign to appear too Dublin-centred. On the first week in May, with over three weeks to voting, Together for Yes embarked on a twelve-day bus tour across Ireland, visiting 40 towns to canvas for a Yes vote. There was great camaraderie on the tour as long-time campaigners Mary Murphy, Ruth Lawlor and Mar Radford joined with the younger women to visit towns and cities supporting the local Together for Yes groups. Regional launches were held in March and April; some, such as Galway and Cork, were big and others very small. Orla and Ailbhe travelled around the country for both the launches and the tour and it gave both of them a great insight into what was happening outside Dublin.

"You could physically see the momentum building for the campaign. By the time the tour came the public were engaging more in the conversation and the feeling was overwhelmingly positive", Orla recalled. In some places there was no launch but a Together for Yes stall would be put up in a town and a meeting held later that night. Many of those groups would have struggled to get venues to agree to host the launch, and there was often tension in advance wondering how many would turn up and would there be protests. Most often there were not.

While the authority of the Catholic Church had waned hugely since the 1983 referendum, it still held more sway in rural rather than urban Ireland. There were a number of instances where the referendum was mentioned from the altar, including at First Holy Communion Masses, given the time of year it was. It felt difficult to gauge just how much influence the Church would have given its emphatic stance on abortion.

Earlier in the year, prior to the referendum being called, the Catholic Primate of All Ireland, Archbishop Eamon Martin, had urged members of the Church to become "missionaries for the cause of life." In a pastoral message for 2018 he had urged Catholics to ignore the strong pressures to remain silent and to speak to relatives, friends, colleagues, and public representatives about the importance of "cherishing the precious gift of life at all times from conception to natural death". Following that, the Catholic bishops said that repealing the Eighth Amendment "would leave unborn children at the mercy of whatever permissive abortion laws might be introduced in Ireland in the future". A further imponderable was added into the mix when a date was announced for the first papal trip to Ireland in nearly 40 years. Pope Francis would not arrive in Ireland until August, after the vote, but there was much speculation that his trip could galvanise Catholic anti-choice feeling.

Orla recalled being on the Together for Yes bus tour as it arrived in Kerry. An event was held in a hotel outside Tralee. It was packed and people were really energised. But a protester did turn up and he was quite aggressive:

> "You know in some ways it almost didn't matter; that wasn't the tone of the meetings. These people had become disconnected from the public. This man came in and he stood up towards the front and took out his phone to record and intimidate the speakers. It was very intrusive with the phone when the speakers were speaking. He wanted to ask questions that were ultimately about giving us a lecture. We were wondering whether to get him removed or not. I think it was me – I was on the top table – I just said, 'Look, if you're finished your questions you're welcome to stay but we're continuing with the meeting.' In the end he left. There was just a totally different vibe going on."

Mullingar was a town where it had been difficult to get a venue to host the local group but a room was eventually located. Anne Gibney from NWCI had volunteered to lead the group. Around twenty chairs were put out and the hope was that these would be filled. Orla remembered:

> "By the time we got up to speak the room was absolutely packed and they were nearly crying in the local group because they knew what that meant.

> It was one of those moments where I just thought how Ireland had changed; this is something so different. And the group was bowled over by the support they got. There was an older man who stood up at that meeting – I'm getting emotional thinking about him – he had campaigned in 1983 against the amendment. And he spoke about the aggressiveness and the insults being thrown at him; I think he actually did say somebody went to hit him at one point during the campaign. He got so emotional and was saying, 'look at all the people around me now and how different this is this time.' It so felt like that."

Another caring aspect of the campaign related to assistance given for childcare. Orla, a single mother to Adam, then eight, remembers this with gratitude. Being a co-director was 24/7 and she remembers that rather than the usual "take off your headphones" she would be telling her son to put them on so he wouldn't be tuned in constantly to what was going on. His school was closed for a week to move premises and she brought him on parts of that bus tour. People were incredible, she said, in that they went out of their way to find things for him to do to keep him entertained:

> "People were just so kind. They would pre-plan it, when they knew I was coming with him. Gráinne was brilliant. I didn't know Gráinne personally before the campaign but we got to know each other well. She would try to organise mums from Parents for Choice to look after Adam in the different places. There was one morning I had to leave for Cork early and Gráinne came out to my house at seven o'clock in the morning and took Adam to school. There's no way I could have gone otherwise."

11

A Female-Led Campaign

It was seen as a pivotal debate in the campaign. On the night it drew 650,000 viewers. In its aftermath RTE would receive 1,277 complaints. It was described by many in Together for Yes as the lowest point of the campaign. Perhaps in the preparation for the *Claire Byrne Live* referendum special the bizarre-sounding proposal that there would be two songs included in the show – one to apparently advocate for a Yes vote, and a second for a No – should have been seen as an early warning sign.

Held on Monday night, 14 May, there was a major build-up to the programme. The communications team had given considerable thought as to who should be on the Yes side and how to play it. Orla was contacted directly by the RTE programme team and asked to appear. She agreed.

"We were told how the show was going to run", said Orla. "There was going to be the songs, a vox pop and then back and forth with panel and audience. The format changed throughout the programme." The final line-up was Orla, Dr Peter Boylan and Sinn Féin leader Mary Lou McDonald on the Yes side. Amy Rose Harte had been concerned that Peter Boylan, who was a big asset to the campaign, was becoming a figure of attack for the No side. However it looked like he would not feature on the upcoming *Prime Time* debate, the second of the RTE debates, so it was decided he should be in the line-up for this major media event.

Opposite was barrister Maria Steen of the Iona Institute, an accomplished television performer; Dr John Monaghan, a retired obstetrician; and Fianna Fáil Waterford TD Mary Butler.

Amy Rose had bad vibes about the programme from early on and was a little nonplussed, she said, to be told during the discussions with RTE that it would be "interesting" and "fun": "Yes that's exactly the words I would have heard at the time ... anyway we had to deal with what we had to do deal with."

In her position at NWCI Orla was an experienced television performer. But this time, in the context of the campaign strategy, the focus of the preparation was on staying on message and role-playing to that effect. By the end Orla felt over-prepared, not having had any quiet time to reflect on what she would like to say, or how to instinctively respond to the programme as it evolved. This was her own usual style of getting ready for a programme.

The debate's presenter, Claire Byrne, began by reminding everyone in studio they were there to discuss a difficult and emotive subject which needed to be approached with care and respect. However it became clear from early on that this debate was not going to shed much light on the subject. Matters quickly got out of hand. There was jeering and whooping and general raucousness from the No side in the audience. For many watching it was like being time-warped back to the awful 1983 campaign.

It was obvious from early on that one of the tactics of the No side was to personally target Peter Boylan. During one fraught exchange, Dr John Monaghan suggested that Dr Boylan should go back to medical school and learn about pregnancy. This came after Dr Boylan said the foetus was not fully developed at twelve weeks.

Independent TD Mattie McGrath, who was in the audience, called Peter Boylan a liar concerning his conclusions on the death of Savita Halappanavar. The Tipperary TD claimed the real story was that the Indian woman had died of "neglect" in the hospital and not because of the Eighth Amendment. Senator Rónán Mullen, who had served on the Oireachtas Committee on the Eighth Amendment, alongside Mattie McGrath, advised those surrounding him in the audience that he himself was a politician and "you can't trust politicians on this issue".

Maria Steen was called a liar by People Before Profit TD Bríd Smith. The Iona Institute member said she took any such accusation very seriously, but the Dáil deputy refused to apologise. Deputy Smith spoke about her own abortion following a crisis pregnancy. Maria Steen said the abortion Bríd Smith had was the sort of 'social abortion' she was warning would happen in Ireland if the Eighth Amendment was repealed.

Claire Byrne implored the participants, at various times, not to call each other liars and to respect each other's point of view. This fell on deaf ears. The Yes side seemed shocked at the tactics being employed and unable to halt the momentum of the other side. Orla remembers one of the most difficult things about the programme was seeing the distressed faces of the members of Terminations for Medical Reasons, as well as Gerry and Gaye Edwards, as they were in the middle of jeering No campaigners.

Amy Rose Harte was backstage with Yvonne Judge from the communications team and Peter Boylan's wife, Jane Mahony. They had notebooks and Amy Rose explained they had been assiduously noting whether those speaking in the audience were Yes or No supporters:

"We were counting quite literally with the notepad, like one Yes GP [doctor], three No GPs. I was picking up the phone to the producer saying 'folks what is going on here? Just to let you know we've now had four, and now five No supporters, and now we – the Yesses – are only on two.' We were operating in real time as best we could. And I was told you're not going to tell us how to produce our own show. We had a good relationship with RTE .... We fully understood they were under pressure from both sides to be balanced. But here it was imbalanced."

Afterwards, members of Terminations for Medical Reasons were very upset in the green room, devastated at what had gone on, remembered Amy Rose. Fatal foetal abnormalities had been mentioned on a few occasions, and despite having spoken in advance to the programme team and outlined what comments they wished to make as audience members, they were not called on at any point during the programme. In the end there was no music either. At the top of the show Claire Byrne said there would be contributions from singer-songwriters Johnny Duhan and Róisín O, but they never appeared. Time ran out.

The programme did knock the wind out of the Together for Yes campaigners in HQ. Although she knew others felt differently, Ailbhe didn't feel it was fatally damaging and that the campaign would learn from it. Mary Lou McDonald, she argued, had "saved the day", while Orla was "held in a pincer movement of silence in a situation she could do nothing about." Peter Boylan had been "under attack".

It was not easy for Orla to go into HQ the next morning:

"I went into the campaign team the next day and I said 'look I feel I have let you down.' I wasn't pretending it was anything else. People were saying I hadn't. It was also hard reading some of the press analysis."

Looking back, she felt there had been high expectations around national media debates, possibly, as was reflected on afterwards, too high, with huge concentration and resources dedicated to them.

There was also the issue of how much control a campaign team can actually have anyway on such things. Then if something goes wrong it can have an immense effect on morale. "Each time we approached these debates as if we could control it all the way through and we couldn't", she said.

In total, 650,000 viewers tuned in at some point during that broadcast, achieving a 35 per cent average audience share – indicating a high level of public interest. Of the 1,277 complaints subsequently received by RTE, just over 90 per cent were related to claims of unfairness towards the Yes side of the campaign.

A letter of complaint was sent to RTE by the co-directors but the station responded robustly to the claims of imbalance. The vitriol evidenced on that show never surfaced to the same extent again during the campaign, and was never evident on the ground, but it did cause the campaign the insecurity of wondering whether it still existed but people were simply not vocalising it.

Sarah Monaghan said while the show was a low point it was a silver-lined one. She had watched it in the boardroom in HQ with Gráinne and the communications team. "We were all watching it and gradually sinking into the end of the table."

But then Claire Brophy from ARC, who was just back from a couple of days on the 'Get Together for Yes' road tour, came in:

> "She hadn't seen the debate and was like 'whoa, what's happened? Has somebody died?' She just said into my ear, 'look I don't care what's after happening. I've been down in rural Ireland for the last three days talking to people in the middle of nowhere, who you would never expect to be engaged with the issue, and they are telling me they are voting Yes.' That didn't even register with me then."

Sinéad Kennedy felt similarly:

> "Afterwards people felt we needed to get moving here, that this wasn't just going to sail through. We needed to be out knocking on doors, and it really was such a shift from people who were

> maybe a little bit complacent or just hadn't fully grasped how
> difficult this was going to be. It was awful for Orla, but a blessing
> in disguise in other ways."

Subsequently, the Broadcasting Authority of Ireland would reject
three complaints made to it concerning an alleged lack of impartiality
and how the debate was moderated. Among other comments, the
Authority's compliance committee said, "the audience participation
was volatile at times; however it was a live debate about an emotive
issue and the robust nature of the debate would be expected and is
consistent with past coverage of referenda debates." A wide range
of views were explored throughout the programme, it added, and
both sides of the debate were afforded the opportunity to present
various viewpoints.

Fallout was guaranteed after such an experience. Campaign
manager Deirdre Duffy said she and Amy Rose Harte had to make
a hard decision the next day on the line-up for an upcoming radio
debate on the Ivan Yates programme *The Hard Shoulder* on Newstalk.
They felt it important to be able to 'neutralise' the effect of barrister
Maria Steen, and halt any gathering momentum for the No side.
But that involved Ailbhe being asked to come off the panel and be
replaced by barrister Gráinne Gilmore. "We needed a lawyer to go
toe-to-toe with Maria Steen", said Amy Rose. "The No side had at
that point opened up a gap on us in terms of scrutinising the legislation. The gap needed to be closed with a very strong legal voice."

Ailbhe acknowledged the rationale behind the decision, and also
that successful campaigning requires tough decisions, but she believed
she had the ability and the nous, given her years of campaigning and
media experience, to have turned in a strong performance:

> "You do have to make decisions in campaigns. Of course we
> needed storytellers, the women who'd had abortions, and
> doctors. Orla and myself should have been out there more,
> talking about women and what women felt and had lived
> through in this country. I did think that there was a voice missing:
> that of a woman campaigner, activist. But although we made

the point at the time, I had to accept the decision made on that occasion because creating a row would have upset the balance of the campaign a couple of weeks out from the referendum, and I would never have done that – it was potentially too damaging. Sometimes in campaigns you have to swallow your pride – and your ego – and hope the decision that's been made will be sound."

Orla said that while the campaign was being led by women they could not fail to see the reaction from the public to the men who were seen as leaders, especially the medics, who got a much more positive public reaction and had their message carried far wider.

One of Amy Rose's stronger memories was walking into that Ivan Yates debate, which was broadcast live from Galway racecourse. "It was very hard. We walked in and there was a place full of No campaigners who were tutting at us as we walked up."

Together for Yes was represented by Fianna Fáil deputy Timmy Dooley, who Amy Rose said was really great in the campaign, and went against the grain as far as most of his party colleagues were concerned. On that day he debated vigorously for the Yes side, along with Dr Mary Higgins and Gráinne Gilmore.

"I remember the producer saying to me we're going to put you all in the room together beforehand and I said absolutely no way, we need to protect our spokespeople. That was purely because tensions were high. But there were moments during that time when you were walking into a room and you weren't quite sure what was going to be the end point of the meeting."

That Claire Byrne show had been the second television debate on RTE. The first was the *Late Late Show* on Friday, 27 April, which had been a very different experience.

Dr Peter Boylan and Dr Mary Favier, a GP and founder member of Doctors for Choice, appeared for the Yes side. When it came to hearing from the audience, Tracey Smith from Co. Mayo spoke of herself and her husband's heart-breaking experience of travelling to Liverpool after receiving a diagnosis of fatal foetal abnormality. Afterwards they received a tracking number for their baby Grace's ashes to be returned. The funeral was a week later; however they did not have the money to return to the UK to attend. Tracey told the audience that a Yes vote would mean that baby Grace could rest in peace.

The Claire Byrne debate, with all the nastiness from the No side, may ultimately have served to assist the Yes argument. But what it also did was give the media an opportunity to criticise the campaign, or talk about a rising sense of pessimism among some Repealers that the campaign was slipping away from them.

Even a few weeks beforehand, on 10 April, in the influential *Irish Times* the newspaper's political editor, Pat Leahy, wrote about the launch of the Together for Yes postering campaign at a photocall in Dublin. The article had the headline: 'Alarm at apparent lack of urgency in Repeal campaign', and the sub-heading 'Well-organised anti-abortion campaign is weeks ahead in its postering and canvassing'. His article pointed out that many of the poles the campaigners and workers decorated with their Yes message already had competing messages – the anti-Repeal posters, with No campaigners beating them well in the poster war. Many of the No posters had already been in place for nearly a fortnight, since the day the referendum was formally called and it became legal to put up posters. For some Repeal supporters, it was a worrying sign that they were weeks behind the anti-Repeal campaigners – in publicity, fundraising, canvassing and implementing a campaign strategy.

Leahy wrote there was a very well-organised, well-funded and committed campaign against the abortion proposal, quoting John McGuirk of the Save the 8th campaign:

> "'Posters aren't that important,' said McGuirk. 'But they are when only one side has them. So we find the "one in five" [the campaign's poster says that one in five babies in the UK are aborted, an interpretation of the UK statistics] thing is coming up on the doors a lot.'"

Observers were agreed, Leahy wrote, that the anti-Repeal side had the better of the early running:

> "Clearly, anti-abortion campaigners have been getting ready for this fight for a long time. But some repealers are wondering why they haven't been preparing with the same urgency. It is not, after all, as if the referendum was a surprise. Privately, some anti-abortion figures say that they are a 'bit mystified' by the repeal campaign so far."

At the Together for Yes HQ the criticism really stung but also felt as if it was coming from 'inside the bubble' of Leinster House, ignoring the movement for change, which campaigners knew – from personal experience and feedback from canvassers – was sweeping the country. That sort of view would continue to be expressed by some right up to polling day: those who would say that the Yes campaign was concentrated too much online, again ignoring the massive extent of the work being done on the ground all over the country, and reluctantly predicting a win, but saying it would likely be a slim one.

Ailbhe said the co-directors recognised that there was a lot of criticism about the posters, but added:

> "Because our funding was so scarce at the start we knew that our posters would have to last and stay relevant throughout the campaign. At that stage we did not think we would be able to afford a second run of posters. Given how long this campaign was I felt it would be no harm for us to go out a bit later with the posters, that people were going to be fed up to the teeth with them by the end."

But Yes supporters wasted no time in strongly feeding back their annoyance to HQ on this issue.

It didn't help that when the posters did go up it took a number of days for the operation, carried out by a distribution company, to be completed around the country. Finally the campaign found, and this was mentioned by a number of people involved, the Yes posters were the subject of dirty tricks and were being deliberately taken down in large numbers.

Gráinne estimated that the No side spent more money on posters than Together for Yes spent on its entire campaign:

"We knew people involved in the business and we tended to hear the numbers of posters that had gone up. Even going out to vote the country had been re-postered for No overnight. Of course it didn't work for them. They were so provocative and so offensive and they so vastly outnumbered ours. Our posters were also being taken down left, right and centre. Volunteers were putting them up and they were gone overnight.

There was also the contentious issue of what went onto the posters. We kept it very simple; we weren't going to debate arguments on corkboard. Ultimately ours supported the much more intensive work on the ground of local campaigners but we did face criticism that they should have been more hard-line. Ultimately though, you'll never get agreement on those kind of decisions. On the second round of posters, I pinned twelve draft posters to the noticeboard in HQ and asked everyone present to gather round and pick three. There was complete disagreement. I took the messaging strategy, the latest research and went off and selected them. That was always my approach, check in with the research, get what feedback could be afforded given the timeframe and adjust the message as needed, but we had developed a very effective core communications strategy and I never strayed too far away from it."

Ailbhe believed the critics were looking at an all-woman team and while they didn't exactly say, 'Ha, ha you fell at the first fence', you could feel that sentiment in some parts of the journalistic milieu:

"That absolutely maddened me. I thought to myself that is not going to happen again. Now that being said, you can't completely control the media. Nobody can, however much they try. But the other thing that happened was that people around the country were thinking, 'we're going lose this', or worse, 'they're going to lose it for us.' In a way though, that most definitely stiffened my backbone no end, I can tell you!"

To Orla's mind, a significant portion of the journalists they were dealing with were:

"... closeted in Dublin in the political world, with politicians, and they were always the most sceptical. It was like they never had a sense of what was on the ground. I remember a few male journalists saying to me 'the twelve weeks is putting people off, people will never agree to it.' Added to that, they couldn't understand having three leaders in the campaign. They always wanted to see one. There was a constant narrative around the campaign being disorganised and lacking leadership, even though they didn't see the signals in the campaign that something totally different was happening throughout the country. Also after the Claire Byrne debate there was a narrative from some quarters of 'oh the politicians need to step in to manage this.'"

Gráinne did feel there was an element of misogyny on the part of some observing the campaign:

"Campaigns generally focus on one or more charismatic individuals to speak for the campaign at all times; our approach was to use a range of people and groups as message carriers. In fact, a lot of the airtime that was counted for the Yes side was interviews with women about their abortion experience without any campaign spokesperson at all. It was interpreted by some as a lack of leadership but actually it was part of our campaign strategy. People found it strange that you would lead a campaign but be prepared to step out of the limelight; you need to be able to set ego aside in favour of the greater good and in a women-led campaign that wasn't an issue."

Sinéad Kennedy's annoyance remains palpable as she remembered the negativity at that time:

> "Basically it was that we could win this – that everyone was on for Repeal – but that the campaign was completely disorganised and didn't know what it was doing. Of course what they were all upset about was that there was no leader apparently, there was no leadership. By that they really meant there was no charismatic man at the centre of the campaign. We had three amazing women – bright, articulate, perfectly capable of putting forward a really strong case – but who didn't really feature an awful lot in the media. The media wanted the doctors and the lawyers out front. I was quite surprised by how little media the three women in some ways did until the very end. It was largely, not exclusively, male doctors. But they liked the male doctors. This is not to disrespect to them, but it's interesting what the media seize upon.
>
> Most of the people in HQ, and all the different team leaders, were women. You go to the grassroots and that was largely women. So you have this campaign that I think an awful lot of journalists did not understand. I think for the most part the people who were writing about it tended to be political correspondents who are so used to seeing things through the lens of Leinster House, through party politics, through the eyes of largely male spokesmen."

Those feelings are strongly echoed by Sarah Monaghan:

> "Remember how it was all about lack of leadership, lack of direction, lack of everything, lack of a campaign? 'Where are they? They're not visible enough. They're not loud enough. There's no clear leadership.' You'll never convince me that it didn't have something to do with it being three female directors leading it and leading it in a different way. It was so successful and so seamless it apparently looked like an absence of leadership and even an absence of a campaign. These were three

women who had compromised a lot and really left ego and a lifetime of history at the doors to work together. And we never knew in the beginning how that would go, but my God, did we pull it off."

For Sarah it echoed somewhat some of the criticisms of the non-hierarchical ARC structure:

"The people who asked the most demeaning questions, in terms of minimising us, were always men who saw our structure as ineffectual time-wasting."

On the plus side, those who were actually involved said there were any number of positives about being involved in an almost exclusively female campaign for the support and camaraderie. Of course men did work on the campaign and it was by no means 'women only'. After all, men were key voters in this referendum.

It was a particularly tricky time for Gráinne. For the first few weeks of the campaign, she was working a half-day at her job while working late into the night to also put in a full day in HQ. She was also finding it increasingly difficult to keep out of the public eye. After a couple of unintended media appearances, Gráinne took to basing herself solely in HQ, driving the backroom, avoiding public events altogether and staying out of the way of any visiting journalists.

It also allowed her to manage the messaging and design of external campaign communications, ensuring the delivery of the communications and messaging strategies through posters, but primarily through advertising. With Noel Whelan and Adam May assigned to an advertising subgroup, she worked with Orla Howard to meet the daily demands for copy. She tracked the themes coming up in the public debates, back from the doors and from the ongoing research and polling. As she explained:

"In the early days of the campaign this was about posters but as the campaign went on and the advertising budget grew, advertising played a much bigger role. We developed an advertising strategy which aligned to the timeframes of the overall campaign strategy, moving soft and concerned Yes voters along a path where they would ultimately vote Yes."

Further research had been done in the middle of the campaign to check that the core message was still on track and to test alternatives. It fed back the confirmation they needed and there was no deviation from the core messaging, although some ads were more sharply tailored to speak to certain voters.

"Advertising, even a full-page broadsheet, is a very limited arena to communicate complex ideas. Everything was distilled to the bare minimum. Messaging reflected what was coming back in the research but adjusted to avoid the campaign coming across as nationalist or further stigmatising abortion. People responded really well to phrases that mentioned concepts like, 'Irish women in our own country' but that would have clearly excluded migrant women, like Savita, and hence we never used them. We moved from an informative approach in the early weeks to bring voters toward a tightly presented dichotomy in the final week, starkly presented on a ballot paper."

In total, Together for Yes placed 95 ads in national daily papers during the campaign.

If there is one memory that stands out for many in this campaign it is that of the constant presence of doughnuts in the kitchen in HQ and the regular devouring of the delicious, high-calorie confectionery. It seems they were constantly being delivered, left in the kitchen, and eaten. One day, to the delight of all, actor Cillian Murphy sent in a cake – chocolate with red icing – which spelled out 'Together for Yes'. The accompanying note read: "Thank you all so much for your hard work on the Together for Yes campaign. Together for change, for equality, for love. Together for Yes! Best Wishes, Cillian Murphy."

People wondered if the *Peaky Blinders* star might have baked it himself. Needless to say, the photo of the celebrity cake played big on social media. On another occasion, author Marian Keyes, a staunch Repeal supporter, sent pizza. Notes of support were regularly sent in, as well as bunches of flowers. Emails would be sent out from HQ to 10,000 subscribers to keep them updated on events and a diligent team, led by Nem Kearns, responded to thousands of queries by phone and email.

In this teeming building packed with full- and part-time volunteers, many of the young women would talk of how they had saved for a year so they could give up work to devote themselves full-time to the campaign. There is always tension in a political campaign, but what those who were there for the duration speak now of is how high the stakes were for people personally, how heavily invested they were and how much a positive result meant. Emotions ran high, and, as in any intense situation, there were tensions or squabbles, but it was remarkable for the lack of open disagreements.

But it was also important to manage that level of emotion and commitment and Deirdre Duffy saw that as part of her job as campaign manager: "It was important to keep everyone calm and focused and not to be letting the enormity of the emotions overtake them."

On Tuesday 10 April, Ailbhe got on a train in Kerry after attending a Together for Yes meeting in that county. There was an email from HQ telling her the crowdfunding effort was being launched that morning at 8.30 a.m. and asking her to donate a few Euros to help get things started. As it happened, the fundraising began on the same day as that *Irish Times* article criticising the pace and running of the campaign. Wifi coverage on the train was intermittent but each time Ailbhe managed to log on she was stunned and delighted to see how quickly the total was rising. The group set an initial target of €50,000 over seven days to fund 5,000 posters across the country. Amazingly, within three hours that target was reached, and then increased to €100,000. Throughout that day the figure kept rising. By midnight an incredible 7,990 people had donated, raising a total of €293,766. The average donation was €37. Ailbhe recalled:

> "It was quite remarkable and it gave not only everyone in Together for Yes at HQ, but everyone around the country, this feeling that they were all involved in this campaign together."

Over the course of the next two days, the overall total continued to increase, with targets being met every few hours, until the final target figure of €500,000 was announced. There was a huge online buzz.

Such was the response it was almost as if people had simply been waiting to be asked. The comments written alongside the donations really told a story reflecting the broad and deep effect of the lack of abortion services in Ireland. Cat, donating €240, wrote that she had just come through a crisis pregnancy:

> "The waiting for an appointment, the stress, the travelling and the pain, in a bed that was not my own, the secrecy, the stigma. It's time we support women and not export them. Trust us."

Ciara Clarke, donating €10, said, "For Savita, thank you and I am sorry." Another, giving €50, simply said, "For Tuam".

One anonymous donation of €2 had the message:

> "I don't have much money – embarrassed at how low this sum is. Thank you all so very much for helping vulnerable women like me."

Another, giving €20, said: "For the women with no names: Ms P, Ms X, Ms A, B and C. Ms D. Repeal the 8th."

Another anonymous message, donating €10, said: "For that time I travelled alone, scared and vulnerable." While a woman who donated €20 said she was the victim of a sex crime who had ended up pregnant and had her life threatened:

> "'I will cut the baby out of you', he said. I travelled. The relief. And then the shame and secrecy. Thank you all for today. Shame is eradicated with compassion".

Sue and John gave €20, saying it was for their grandchildren: "May they never suffer fear over a pregnancy." "In memory of Caoimhe, yet another loved baby left behind in a UK hospital", said a message with an anonymous donation of €20.

There was humour too. In response to women being told to control their urges for the 'devil's sausage', one woman gave €50, explaining: "Because I've enjoyed #devilssausage on so many occasions."

€300 was donated by Elizabeth, saying she lived abroad and felt really guilty she could not get home to vote and hoped the donation would be used to persuade a few more people who wouldn't otherwise to come out to vote.

In her message, LeeAnne, donating €20, appeared to summarise the feelings of many others:

> "For all the unmarried women who have suffered in Ireland. For future generations of Irish women. For being on the right side of history. For trusting women. For basic human rights. For proper medical care. For choice. For respect. For Repealing the 8th."

The success of the crowdfunding was clearly important for the money it raised, but every bit as important for the morale boost it provided to the campaign, adding to the sense that there was huge support all over the country and people were motivated and determined that this referendum would be passed.

By the end of the referendum campaign, 30,000 supporters donated a total of €1.5 million, including €750,000 from two crowdfunds. As well as that, 250 events, attended by 16,000 people, were held. These raised €200,000. When it came to those controversial Together for Yes posters, by voting day on 25 May almost 29,000 had been put up around the country in 19 different designs.

The campaign's fundraising team, which worked in a windowless office in HQ, was led by social justice activist Denise Charlton with the advice and support of Ask Direct, a fundraising and campaigning strategy company, which had previously worked with the Coalition to Repeal the Eighth. Denise had vast experience in this area and had honed her skills in the marriage equality referendum. As well as the crowdfunding she drove the money-raising effort in diverse areas, including fun runs and packs supplied for people to have fundraisers and conversations in their own homes, as well as contact and relationship building with individual donors.

The campaign was exceptionally tough physically for Ailbhe, who had developed a bad back the previous November. From then on it kept deteriorating. She had an MRI on New Year's Eve 2017, which revealed the extent of the problem:

> "I had treatment during the campaign which actually made it worse, and of course it was exacerbated by stress. Walking was difficult; sitting was difficult; standing was just about bearable; and driving was a nightmare. Lying down was fine but there wasn't any time for that, so I just had to keep going. There was one particular day I remember coming in in the morning. I had a busy day ahead, and I was in a lot of pain. I just burst into tears but luckily I met Carl Hayden, who worked in the campaign, at the door. And he said 'right, you're in a taxi now, home for the day.'"

After that, Gráinne arranged for her neighbour Dermo to volunteer as campaign driver for Ailbhe and he became an integral part of the team.

As the weeks went on, opinion polls continued to show a strong lead for the Yes side, though that lead had slipped since the start of the campaign. One of the interesting things about the Together for Yes canvassing teams around the country was how they appeared to seamlessly bring together members of different political parties, some of very different persuasions, all under the same banner going door-to-door to ask for a Yes vote.

On a national level it was a bit more complicated. The Government's position was that it supported repeal of the Eighth Amendment. Taoiseach Leo Varadkar was seen to take a more backseat approach and allowed the Minister for Health, Simon Harris, to spearhead the Government campaign. It is widely acknowledged that he did a very good job. There was regular contact with the Minister's office to ensure both sides kept each other updated and to ensure there weren't any campaign scheduling clashes. Minister for Culture, Heritage and the Gaeltacht Josepha Madigan was appointed to coordinate the Fine Gael campaign, but did not have a huge profile on the issue. Early on in the campaign, the co-directors had attended a meeting in Fine Gael headquarters. They did not come away with the impression that a huge effort was being put in at party level, especially when they were told no more than €100,000 would be spent on the campaign by the party. Fine Gael offered their elected representatives referendum posters, on which they could have their names printed, but the uptake was very low.

Bets were still being hedged clearly, but the Together for Yes campaign recognised the need for a level of coordination with the Government party, and Fine Gael held a high-profile launch of its referendum campaign at which the Taoiseach spoke.

Given its internal divisions on abortion, the Fianna Fáil party operated on a more individual level in terms of supporting the campaign, but there was strong support from leader Micheál Martin and his chef de cabinet, Corkwoman Deirdre Gillane.

The Labour Party, which had opposed the insertion of the Eighth Amendment in the Constitution in 1983, was consistent in its backing for Repeal, and people like Senator Ivana Bacik, a long-standing pro-choice campaigner, and Deputy Jan O'Sullivan played an important public role. The political parties and independents further on the left, such as People Before Profit, the Socialist Party and Independents 4 Change, were unequivocally pro-choice and stood fully behind Repeal. They put in a huge effort to get the referendum passed both in the Oireachtas and in mobilising and canvassing around the country.

In general it had been more difficult to engage men in the campaign and this was evident with the crowdfunding, which involved a majority of women contributing, as did the make-up of the canvassing groups. In preparation for the final week of the campaign, NWCI did a focus group with men. These would have been men who were partners of people in the campaign, so they were already engaged. But one of the things they said was that they didn't like talking about the issue when they were out, like in the pub with friends.

"I wish this referendum was just over. I'm going to go out and vote for it, but I don't want to keep talking about it", was the type of attitude they would have had. The statistics from social media also showed that men were not engaging as much as the campaign would have wanted.

"So we developed strong social media messages to build empathy and to encourage men to think about the women in their lives who may have had an abortion or who might need one in the future. This messaging was also carried through into the 'Who needs your Yes' initiative by NWCI in the final 10 days", explained Orla. Invited to use the Twitter hashtag #whoneedsyouryes, people responded in their droves to collectively share intimate and emotional feelings, saying they were voting for mothers, sisters, daughters, friends, or their younger selves.

If Irish women had left unspoken for so long their experiences of travelling abroad in secrecy for abortions, the Together for Yes campaign would prove to be a dam burst in terms of decades of stories, most of them harrowing, finally being aired in public.

The telling of these personal stories was a vital part of the campaign, especially when it came to a contentious referendum and that 'concerned centre' who identified with and were moved by these personal experiences when they heard them. This had already proven key in the marriage equality referendum. Those stories were also welcomed with open arms by the media, who knew that readers, listeners and viewers were far more likely to engage with someone speaking directly of their own experiences. Former RTE producer Yvonne Judge, who had come on board with the Coalition before Christmas, set up and oversaw the establishment of the Together for Yes 'Storylab', where these accounts would be gathered. "We knew what drives media editors and producers; personal stories are gold", recalled Yvonne, who now runs her own communications company. "As I knew from my time in RTE, the motto was 'Keep them listening, late for work in their cars'. Crucially, we were telling personal stories as evidence to back up the medical facts."

During the Together for Yes campaign at least 54 personal stories were told on radio, TV, in print and online. The media always wanted something 'fresh' but the campaign was very conscious that even telling the story once was a huge emotional effort for those involved. Looking back on the campaign of the No side, Yvonne estimated they had up to eight personal stories which were often repeated. Of the 54 personal Yes stories told, 28 referred to fatal foetal abnormalities, and 26 referred to personal abortion stories concerning those who had travelled alone, were taking pills alone now, or had been abused, suffered depression or were raped.

"These personal stories reached hundreds of thousands of listeners, readers and viewers", said Yvonne. "We doubt there is a voter that did not hear or read at least one of the Together for Yes personal stories. At the beginning of the campaign they did not know how many women would be willing to talk. "We had a duty of care to these incredible women to prepare and protect them. We insisted on pre-recording. Anonymity was assured."

Gerry Edwards, who had spoken at the Together for Yes launch along with his wife, Gaye, was the first person Yvonne rang in early February 2018. Gerry became a national spokesperson for Together for Yes. He was the one man among ten women who gathered for a media preparation session in HQ in the first week of March, where they all listened to each other tell their stories, all different, all personal. Looking back, Yvonne said it was more like a counselling session.

RTE Radio One's flagship current affairs programme, *Morning Ireland*, carried five personal stories; all ran at 8.45 a.m., the optimum audience time when there were up to 400,000 people listening to stories of fatal foetal abnormalities, pills and sepsis.

The *Pat Kenny Show* on Newstalk ran three personal stories, with an audience of 170,000 each. Yvonne remembers one unidentified woman who told her story of taking abortion pills. She featured on a package on RTE Radio's *News At One* programme. During it she said, "I am not an activist; I don't have blue hair; I make sandwiches for the local GAA."

RTE Radio One's *Drivetime* show ran a series of personal stories from both sides by Philip Boucher-Hayes. The programme begins at 4.30 p.m. on weekdays and these stories were carried at the later time of 6.15 p.m., when the audience is around 150,000. But the fact that it was a series running from the first week of March 2018 meant they became significant to the audience and people began to listen out for them.

Regional radio preferred the debate format and that sector was difficult to penetrate, Yvonne recalled, but eventually as the personal stories resonated nationally, they did run them. Tabloid newspapers insisted on photos so the issues around anonymity meant the campaign found them almost impossible to penetrate. Many regional newspapers, recalled Yvonne, flatly refused to engage with Together for Yes for months, and one entire regional group refused to do so right to the end. Hundreds of women also told their stories through the very successful 'In Her Shoes' Facebook platform, and the Everyday Stories project.

As polling day drew closer, the campaign momentum just kept building. Two former Attorneys General, John Rogers SC and Michael McDowell SC, along with former Supreme Court judge Catherine McGuinness, made a statement calling for a Yes vote at an event organised by Lawyers for Yes. A national database of signatures from lawyers who supported a Yes vote was revealed. The campaign kept rolling out the different support bases with Parents for Yes, Grandparents for Yes, Men for Yes, Midwives for Yes and even Dogs for Yes – owners could deck out their dogs in Yes bandanas.

A number of new groups of professionals had also formed and joined the Together for Yes platform, making a total of 97. They included the Irish Association of Social Workers, Engineers for Yes, Dentists for Yes, Psychiatric Nurses for Yes, Farmers for Yes, Writers for Yes, Adopted People for Yes, Scientists for Yes, and Inclusion Ireland, all representing hundreds of thousands of members.

Concern had been mounting about the increasing number of online ads relating to the referendum that were appearing, especially since they could potentially involve interference from outside the country in a space which was unregulated and where electoral harm had been shown to have been done in the 2016 US Presidential election and the Brexit referendum in the UK. Campaign ads appeared in people's feeds but there was no way of knowing exactly who had paid for them. Print and broadcast ads were subject to strict rules but online ads were unregulated.

Then just over two weeks to voting day, Facebook, in a surprise move, announced it would no longer accept foreign advertisements relating to the referendum. Google, taking it a step further, then announced that it would ban all campaign advertising also. The moves were welcomed by Repeal campaigners but incensed those on the No side.

One of the most memorable aspects of the campaign was the Together for Yes merchandise, a key driver of profile with badges, pins, stickers, tote bags, T-shirts and Repeal jumpers. They became a way for supporters to identify each other, whether on a city street where support was visibly swelling or in a small village where it was a wonderful lift to see a fellow supporter proud to publicly proclaim their wish for a Yes vote, or give someone the courage to wear their own badge tomorrow.

Regional groups were given merchandise and it could also be bought online. A number of pop-up shops were opened, including two in Cork, and one each in Galway and Kildare. But the main retail outlet was a shop in Temple Bar which opened in early May. For Gráinne, who had planned a campaign shop from the beginning and recruited friends and ARC volunteers to set up and run the operation:

> "... it was also about creating a physical access point between the public and the campaign, a place for supporters to grab a bunch of badges for friends and family, or for someone with questions to pop in and have a chat with a campaign volunteer.

> It showed the campaign as outgoing, engaging and transparent. We weren't going to hide away."

Black jumpers with the word 'Repeal' emblazoned across the chest had been designed by Anna Cosgrave in 2016 when she set up the Repeal Project. At that time when she asked friends to wear them they were nervous about doing so, but by referendum day the jumpers were the iconic symbol of the Repeal movement.

ARC had partnered with Anna and relaunched the black Repeal jumpers on its own website while for the referendum campaign Sarah Monaghan worked tirelessly with Anna to bring out a new round of coloured jumpers for Together for Yes. In the end 6,000 Repeal jumpers, retailing at €25 each, were sold, as well as 7,000 Together for Yes T-shirts. A quarter of a million badges and 150,000 stickers were distributed.

The jumpers were launched at the opening of the Temple Bar shop and there was a queue all the way down the street of people wanting to buy them in the new array of colours. "It was something a bit lighter and colourful and the media loved it", said Sarah Monaghan:

> "It was as close to a fluff piece in the abortion referendum as you were going get, so it was great. We also had celebrities in buying them. Of course merchandise isn't just about making money; in fact in most campaigns it's not about making money. You might break even. It's about making the support visible. It probably has more value in terms of that than it has financially. But the Repeal jumpers were special. You'll never replicate that in terms of a brand which had been building for years."

As 25 May approached fast, the canvassing became even more high-profile. The weekend before the vote Health Minister Simon Harris was joined by the then Master of the National Maternity Hospital, Dr Rhona Mahony, for a high-profile canvas of the Leinster–Munster Pro-14 semi-final at the RDS. Sunday newspaper headlines were positive, with the *Sunday Times* reading: 'Urban surge set to carry the day for repeal vote'. The results of a poll there and one in the *Sunday Business Post* pointed towards a win.

On the Monday of that last week, Simon Harris would pull no punches in a press conference when he said the opposition of the Catholic Church to social change needed to be challenged and scrutinised. He fully respected the Church's right to express their opposition to abortion but disagreed with its view on this issue, on marriage equality, and on contraception.

Then on the Tuesday night the third RTE debate took place, this time on *Prime Time*. The controversy there began even before the programme aired. That day the Love Both spokeswoman, Cora Sherlock, pulled out of the programme, on which she was to be joined by then Sinn Féin TD Peadar Tóibín in calling for a No vote. Health Minister Simon Harris and Professor Mary Higgins had agreed to argue for a Yes vote and had been preparing together. However RTE was told on the day that Cora Sherlock was not available and that Maria Steen of the Iona Institute would be in her place. In response RTE took a strong line, saying it would not agree to this change, that Maria Steen had already appeared on the *Claire Byrne Live* debate. The No side claimed to be incensed, but the national broadcaster refused to budge.

Campaigner manager Deirdre Duffy said it had been a consistent feature of the approach to debates by the No side to pull out or to change personnel late in the day. In the end the line-up was two men – Simon Harris, wearing a Tá Together for Yes badge, against Peadar Tóibín.

In the line of the night, the Minister told his opponent, "We're standing here with the luxury of being two men who will never experience a crisis pregnancy", adding that his opponent was ignoring the reality facing those women.

Peadar Tóibín said the Government proposals were "breathtakingly extreme". Simon Harris said, "we're all one in Ireland until you're a pregnant woman" and then it's a very lonely place. This was a far less heated affair than the previous debate, with good performances on both sides, but the Minister was acknowledged to have delivered very effectively for the Yes side.

The following night the then TV3 channel hosted a debate chaired by Pat Kenny. Maria Steen did make an appearance there, along with Senator Rónán Mullen. The Yes side was represented by Amnesty director Colm O'Gorman and the Minister for Employment Affairs and Social Protection, Regina Doherty.

Showing how the No side had attempted to redirect in the previous few days, attempting to make up ground, Maria Steen nodded to the difficulty of the 'hard cases', bringing in the idea that while twelve weeks was too extreme there should be abortion in some, very limited, instances.

That TV3 debate was most notable for the appearance of DJ and presenter Saoirse Long, who spoke very movingly from the audience about travelling to the UK for an abortion:

"I thought long and hard about what I did. And the decision I made was the right decision for me and I should have been looked after in my own country."

There was significant online comment at Rónán Mullen's reaction after the young woman spoke about the aftermath of the abortion and being away from home. "Walking around Birmingham for six hours with a hot water bottle against me, alone, walking around a country and a city I don't know, waiting for a plane home again because I was forced out of this country", Ms Long said.

"You deserve love and respect despite what you may have done", Senator Mullen told her.

During that broadcast the Taoiseach tweeted that he would be voting Yes on Friday "for all the women in my life, my mum, my sisters and my female friends, including the friend who told me about her own abortion. I think they all deserve safe and compassionate care here and at home."

During the day in HQ, Aoife Cooke, a former member of ARC who had travelled back from Australia for the campaign, had been creating an audio archive. She went around recording everyone's experiences and thoughts on the campaign and why it was so important to them. "You knew when someone had been talking to

Aoife because their eyes were red. Everyone was crying. It was very emotional in the last few days" recalled Sinéad Kennedy. "I'm not usually someone who cries in public but Aoife started talking about how important it was and there I was bawling. I was mortified."

12

A Stunning Victory

As voting day drew closer the #hometovote hashtag began to trend on social media, with people posting messages and photos as they made their way home from places as far flung as Buenos Aires, Vietnam, Australia and the US. For a number of them it was funding efforts, such as those coordinated by Abroad for Yes, that paid for their journey. The initiative matched funds with people who needed them to travel through Facebook. The London-Irish Abortion Rights Campaign had launched hometovote.com, a global campaign which produced two videos featuring the Irish diaspora arriving home from all over the world. At this point the tension and excitement was really building.

The final Together for Yes press conference was held two days before the vote on 25 May. The room in HQ was packed with print, broadcast and online journalists. At that point there was almost saturation coverage of the referendum, with attention not just at home but also major coverage in the international media.

In line with the Together for Yes communications strategy, the press conference concentrated on one aspect of the debate and comprehensively explored it, offering clear medical and legal expert opinion from the panel as well as personal stories. The media event focused on the abortion pill, which had become such a big talking point of the campaign, and the fact that women all over Ireland were taking it illegally and often without support, and they felt unable to visit a doctor should a complication arise.

Dublin woman Elaine Bedford told of how her daughter Kate, who has type 1 diabetes and polycystic ovaries, had taken the abortion pill and of the traumatic impact the experience had on her and the family. Kate had become pregnant unexpectedly and decided to take an abortion pill because continuing the pregnancy would have meant further risk to her health:

> "She took the tablets at home with me – it was terrifying. I put her to bed. I was bringing in hot water bottles. My daughter was in agony and bleeding and as she was losing consciousness, I couldn't lift the phone to tell the doctors."

She said the hell continued for three days, with pain and bleeding, while she and Kate's boyfriend took shifts to look after her:

> "But no doctor. I should have been able to go to the doctor about my daughter. We had no idea how the diabetes would affect the pills – or her. I completely stand over Kate's decision and also any other girl in Ireland who is put in that position. My heart goes out to every one of those women – it's not cut and dried, nobody can judge anybody .... That's why I am speaking out for my girl and for any girl. And it's why I'll be voting yes this Friday May 25th to look after our daughters as a country."

At times Elaine was overcome with emotion telling her story and was assisted by Sinn Féin leader Mary Lou McDonald, who was also at the top table along with senior counsel Noel Whelan. After listening to the story he said he would happily defend Kate against the fourteen-year sentence for taking abortion pills, the term in the statute books for such action, and he knew know no jury would convict.

The Sinn Féin leader said she had a teenage girl herself, and she could imagine no situation:

> "... worse for my girl than that she should ever find herself in such a lonely position – that she would feel forced or compelled, left with no other option but to take these pills on her own and without the protection of the law or the protection of medicine. I take a very simple view as a person and a politician and a leader that if I feel this way about my girl, I extend the same sentiment to everybody else's daughters or sisters or mothers or our neighbours or our friends."

Sinéad Kennedy remembered how in the last few days politicians seemed to be constantly dropping into HQ – a real indicator they believed the Yes side was set for a win. They wanted photos and selfies. There was a photocall with politicians near the Pepper Canister Church which had such a good all-party political turnout it was a further indication of the way confidence was rising:

> "I remember Jim O'Callaghan from Fianna Fáil was coming into HQ and we were having a meeting. And the others turned to me, and said, 'now you behave' as if I was going to attack him. [She laughs at the memory.] So I said, 'look, I am a Marxist, but I'm not rude! I just won't be fawning over them. I'll just say hello and whatever.'"

On the weekend before the vote, in a key intervention, the late Savita Halappanavar's father and mother called for a Yes vote. The video was released by *Irish Times* journalist Kitty Holland on Twitter on the Saturday night. Andanappa and his wife, Mahadevi, holding a framed picture of Savita, urged people to remember their daughter when it came time to vote:

> "My dear brothers and sisters of Ireland, I am Savita's unfortunate father, Andanappa. Speaking on the historic event of repeal of the Eighth Amendment. The day of the people of the island who now know the pain and the memory of our loving daughter Savita. No family in future should have to undergo what we have gone through, the worry and sorrow that's still persistent in our hearts even after some six years. The life that Savita had, she had a very long life to lead, but it was cut down mercilessly there.
>
> Savita loved the people of Ireland. Lots of people say that Savita's death hurt the entire Irish society. I strongly feel that the younger daughters of Ireland should not have the fate of Savita. I hope that people in Ireland will remember the fate of our daughter Savita on the day of the referendum and vote Yes so that what happened to us won't happen to any [other] families."

Savita's father added that by doing this voters would be paying a great debt to the departed soul of his daughter.

The *Sunday Independent* ran an article on the video on page two the next morning and as the day went on it gained huge traction, not just in Ireland but also abroad. This was an important moment for the campaign on the last weekend before the vote. It was not the first intervention from Savita's parents. In April, speaking to Kitty Holland, they said they had not known of the referendum vote and hoped people would vote Yes.

All during the campaign the Cervical Check controversy had raged, casting doubts over the effectiveness of the national cervical smear programme. It put a huge amount of pressure on the Government at the time, and affected its popularity. It was also a significant moment, not just for politicians but for the public, who were appalled by what had been revealed. But it also appeared to boost the campaign, highlighting as it did the attitude to women's healthcare in Ireland. Terminally ill Vicky Phelan brought the scandal to light when she went public after she won a court case against a US laboratory which carried out testing over the alleged misreading of her smear tests under the CervicalCheck programme. A review carried out after she had been diagnosed with cervical cancer uncovered that her earlier smear test under the screening programme was a false negative. However this was not communicated to her by the HSE for three years. The fallout from the Vicky Phelan case resulted in one of the most significant health controversies ever experienced in this country. Only days after she stood on the steps of the Four Courts, following the settlement of her case, it became clear that hundreds of women, who similarly to Vicky also had cancer, had also not been told that an audit was conducted that revised the results of their earlier, negative smear tests.

Dr Cliona Loughnane, NWCI women's health coordinator, contacted Vicky to discuss her perspective on the referendum. On 17 May Vicky came out in support of a Yes vote. She said she believed women should have a choice. Using the #whoneedsyouryes hashtag on Twitter, she said:

> "If we really want women to be placed at the centre of their own care, vote Yes to allow us to make the choice about our own care."

On Friday, 25 May, referendum day, the front-page headline on the *Irish Independent* was, 'Yes camp fearful of "silent No" vote'. Political editor Kevin Doyle wrote underneath: "A large silent No is the only factor that could derail the repeal of the Eighth Amendment as the country goes to the polls". But the article went on to say that Yes campaigners in the abortion referendum were "confident they had won over enough people" to secure victory in the key vote.

The previous day in the same newspaper, pictured with his wife, Ruth, and three young daughters, Tánaiste Simon Coveney, who had so publicly wavered on the issue, wrote of why he would vote Yes. His engagement with doctors and women who had told him their stories of vulnerability, isolation and crisis in pregnancy had left him in no doubt as to the need for change. "I was content in my view until I really took the time to confront it and was in turn confronted by reality", he said.

On the same day the *Irish Times* editorial concluded:

> "With a Yes vote, we can reject a worldview that relegates a woman's bodily autonomy below the right of the State to tell her it knows best. We can bring an end to the secrecy and the shame. And we can embrace a more generous idea of the State itself. Repeal the Eighth."

Throughout the campaign Together for Yes had adopted a dual social media strategy to mobilise the base and to convince undecided voters. The social media campaign was led by Sarah Clarkin, NWCI communications officer. As she recalled:

> "We had to ensure that our social media was an engaging space for our supporters around the country, but it was also crucial that we reached beyond our base and that our social media was also informative and engaging for undecided voters. It sounds obvious now, but at the time we were very concerned with getting the balance right. There was a real risk that in trying to target everyone, our pages would appeal to no one."

The social media team of Sarah Clarkin, ARC's Emma Allen, and Linda Kavanagh developed appropriate content for each platform that Together for Yes would engage on, namely Twitter, Facebook and Instagram. While the messaging would be the same across all platforms, the audiences varied, so the content needed to be tailored. Twitter was heavily made up of supporters and the base, while they could engage heavily with undecided voters on Facebook. Instagram was used to engage the younger voters, while Instagram Stories were used to show the background work of the campaign and the canvassing teams across the country. Instagram was particularly effective for the early 'Register to Vote' effort and the later 'Get Out the Vote' stages.

On Facebook the strategy was to equip volunteers and supporters with information and personal stories to share with friends and family to encourage them to vote Yes. Initially the strategy was to focus purely on organic content, but throughout April paid promotion was also used. In April, on Facebook, an average of 84,000 people per day were reached through sharing and a further 72,000 per day with paid promotion. This was a great opportunity to test the messaging against different audiences.

By mid-campaign Twitter had become a crucial tool in setting a media narrative. Campaigns such as #Men4Yes ended up working as complementary social and traditional media campaigns. Instagram Stories often took on a life of their own, with the social media team managing a WhatsApp group, with members from every local group sharing their canvassing photos, and these were then uploaded onto Instagram Stories. Sarah Clarkin remembered:

> "Some of the nicest messages we received in the campaign were from supporters who told us that the last thing they did every night before they went to sleep was to look through our Instagram Stories at the hundreds of canvassers around the country. It gave people so much belief."

Video was also used across all social media channels, particularly Facebook. Some of the best performing pieces of content in mid-campaign, before the Together for Yes brand was fully established, were newspaper articles. Pieces from politicians and public figures, such as Fianna Fáil leader Micheál Martin and soccer pundit and psychotherapist Richie Sadlier performed very well among the Together for Yes base, and also among undecided voters.

The Together for Yes website was a key communications tool for the campaign. It was coordinated by Silke Paasche, NWCI head of communications. There were a few phases to the website, reflected in particular on the homepage. Upon launching the main aim was to present the campaign as a credible, trustworthy voice, to highlight the large number of organisations that had signed up, and to provide clear information about how the campaign would be funded.

At the end of the campaign it focused on the closing arguments. Anticipating an increase in the number of undecided voters searching for information in the final days, the homepage was redesigned to focus exclusively on featuring the main arguments and the most convincing videos of the campaign, as well as practical information about voting.

As the campaign entered the final weeks the numbers began to rise incredibly. Instagram Stories were viewed by 4,000 people every day. Three million Irish people were reached, multiple times, on Facebook in the final week. On the day of the vote over two million Irish people saw something from Together for Yes in their newsfeed.

On Twitter Together for Yes tweets were viewed 9.2 million times. In May mentions grew to 45,000, and impressions doubled to 20.7 million. A celebrity endorsement video posted on 6 May, featuring, amongst many others, Saoirse Ronan, Cillian Murphy, Hozier, Liam Cunningham, Maria Doyle Kennedy, Pauline McLynn, James Nesbitt and Tom Vaughan Lawlor was viewed 1.3 million times alone. As Sarah Clarkin explained:

"Our social media had something for everyone. For campaigners who wanted to see what was happening around the country, we had canvassing photos. For real stories about how the Eighth Amendment had harmed women, we had moving videos. If you wanted to donate or volunteer, you could contact us and we would make sure you found the right person. It was a gateway to the campaign for everyone, regardless of what level of support they could give."

At the final campaign event, on the day before polling, Together for Yes called on the Irish people to turn out to vote in what would be a 'once-in-a-generation opportunity'. The co-directors were joined by a group of Together for Yes supporters in Merrion Square Park, along with a giant circular YES badge for a high-profile photo opportunity. It was also the day of a Cabinet photocall asking people to vote Yes. Orla and Ailbhe joined this photo opportunity and both thought afterwards the high turnout of senior politicians was a clear sign that they were confident of a positive referendum result.

A week before the poll the campaign had launched a digital tool which would remind people to go out and vote Yes the following Friday. Once you signed up it sent a free reminder text the morning of polling day. It also allowed people to plan how to get to the polling station.

A real encouragement had been news from the Department of Housing, Planning and Local Government that more than 118,000 people had been added to the supplementary voter register for the referendum – the official register of new voters since the previous register was published – indicating a big surge in young people wanting to vote, most likely for Yes.

For the last week, Laura Harmon's mobilisation team were involved in the 'Get Out the Vote' phase of the campaign. Mary Coogan, who had worked as volunteer coordinator in HQ, joined a team of ARC volunteers who were assigned to implement the turnout strategy, which had been developed in the weeks coming up to the vote. The number of people who could be motivated to go and vote Yes on voting day would be crucial. Supporters and canvassers were reminded of the importance of being a visible, as well as a colourful and positive, presence on the streets, with Yes stickers and badges. They were asked to return to canvas strong Yes areas to remind people to vote that Friday. As Mary remembered:

> "It was the little winks and thumbs up at seven in the morning when people were on the way to work when they saw your Yes badge. At that stage everyone was mad for badges. There was a team of us, and we each had maybe seven or eight groups that we called every day around the country to check in with them and see how they were getting on. At that stage it was just like 'okay guys we're nearly there. You're doing everything right. We're not going to engage in any negativity. Just hold your head up and keep smiling and walk away.' At that stage people were obviously tired."

Ailbhe remembered droves of people leaving HQ to go on super canvasses at Dublin Luas and DART stations. She remembered being on one in particular herself with Laura Harmon, former USI president and now leadership coordinator with NWCI, on St Stephen's Green. It was rush hour. People were running past, dashing and saying things like "You're grand, you're fine", "I'll take one for a friend; thanks, brilliant." On the one hand Ailbhe said she was worried that this was just Dublin but she also felt in her bones it was going to be a win:

> "I was without emotion. I was just working. I was an automaton. You have to keep doing it because you can't allow yourself to be excited or anxious. But I noticed all these things and thought 'this is fantastic' – and got on with the job."

By that point there were daily videos going out to campaigners on social media, usually from the co-directors, trying to keep energy levels up as the finishing point was in sight. These short recordings would finish with a collectively intoned "We are Together for Yes", which usually made everyone involved laugh.

Orla recalls the morning walk to HQ in the final week and how phenomenal it was to see the increasing numbers of campaigners at Luas stations in Dublin: "There was such a positive feeling with members of the public going out of their way to speak with campaigners and say 'I'm voting Yes.'"

Sarah Monaghan never felt sure it was going to be a win even though the canvas returns and the feedback from local groups were so positive:

> "We were getting feedback in the last two weeks or so, from the likes of Éilís Murphy in Co. Clare, who had set up the most wonderful ARC group and whose Together for Yes canvasses were now coming back with something in the region of 55 per cent and 60 per cent Yes. These were people I knew for years and we'd ring them and say: 'Are you sure you're tallying right?' They'd tell us that of course they knew how to tally! But it was too

surreal to believe, and too important to even let yourself believe it. We just kept on with that mantra of 'Complacency is what will topple this campaign.' So right up until the final moment, we were all out on the last day, every one of us, doing the high-visibility campaign work."

The digital team had been seeing a solid Yes majority for weeks, even when undecideds were included. A selection of returns from the final few days shows just how positive the figures were – Arklow, Co. Wicklow showed a 58 per cent Yes, 23 per cent No and 19 per cent Maybe. Athlone, Co. Westmeath was 56.25 per cent Yes, 18.75 per cent No and 25 per cent Maybe. Dublin Bay South was 73.04 per cent Yes, 14.78 per cent No, 12.17 per cent Maybe. Kerry was 45.27 per cent Yes, 22.97 per cent No, 31.76 per cent Maybe. And Sligo was 66.67 per cent Yes, 13.89 per cent No and 19.44 per cent Maybe.

Lee Daly from the digital team said that from looking at the canvas returns it was impossible not to feel upbeat:

"The facts were constantly positive so I never doubted that it would be won on the basis of the numbers. Personally I was conscious that I came into the campaign late and that I'm a man, so I saw my goal as giving people reasons to be positive and the numbers were consistently positive. It felt like such a privilege to be there; everyone was really great at their job."

On the night before voting Lee sent his final report in an email to senior campaign figures, saying that, as had been the trend throughout the campaign, it was hard to see a path to victory for No based on canvas returns. Yes had a large majority in the returns in urban areas, at least parity in larger towns, and were north of 40 per cent even in the most rural areas.

A silent No would have to be very large, he wrote, and combined with a similar sized overestimation of their Yes vote, for Yes to not reach 51 per cent at least. The fact that the returns echoed the polls and had trended upwards continuously was also encouraging.

He included a sample from the last few days of returns and attached a graph giving returns from the previous few days from all over the country, urban and rural. Out of a total of 1,803 people canvassed it showed 60.91 per cent Yes, 20.17 per cent No and 18.92 per cent Maybe, remarkably close to the final result.

On the day before the vote there was a meeting of all the campaign team and the co-directors. Each of the co-directors gave final words of encouragement to the team. Orla got emotional that morning recalling the words of Mark Garrett when the strategy was being formed:

"He said earlier in the campaign when we were developing the strategy, 'you want to reach the end of the campaign where you feel like there was just nothing else you could have done.' And I remember saying to everyone on the team that no matter what the vote was, over the last weeks we have all done everything we could possibly have done to achieve a Yes vote tomorrow. We were all emotional because of our anticipation of the next day; we all knew how much was at stake for women and we were all exhausted."

Gráinne and Orla Howard had been flat out for the last ten days of the campaign. As the funds came in the advertising budget grew and demands for ad copy with it. On the final weekend before the vote there were two full-page ads in the national newspapers, several specifically targeted at men, arising out of the focus group research, in order to increase the male Yes vote. With the No side also pushing medical spokespeople out front and centre, they worked with designer Fiona Hanley to capture the scale of medical support for the Yes vote. An entire list of all the doctors who had signed up to support Doctors for Yes was published as a full-page ad, with the tagline: 'As doctors we make difficult decisions every day. 1,517 of us are agreed on this one.' For the final day something completely different from what they had done to date was produced: the bright colours and branding were dropped and instead a sombre picture of Savita was used with the simple message 'Never again'.

Gráinne had also been working with Sarah Monaghan to plan and manage ARC's referendum campaign. Given its skills at fundraising over the previous years, the ARC war chest meant the group was able to spend close to €400,000 on the campaign. ARC decided to run a campaign to complement Together for Yes. It particularly wanted to support regional groups and campaigners to deliver the message locally, something ARC felt fitted well with its ethos and grassroots philosophy. It proposed to partner with Together for Yes on two large-scale promotional projects, both requiring early planning and investment, and both well outside of the planned Together for Yes budget at the time.

The first was a large nationwide advertising campaign in local newspapers. For the last two weeks of May over 50 regional newspapers carried two well-placed half-page ads for Together for Yes, sponsored by ARC. The second ARC project was to post a full-colour Together for Yes booklet to every household in Ireland at a cost of over €200,000.

The ARC-sponsored booklet was a huge investment for the group but would reinforce the work of local canvassers on the doors and reach households beyond the reach of some of the local canvassing groups. By the end of the campaign 6.5 million Together for Yes leaflets and booklets had been distributed. As ARC continued to bring in donations during the campaign, it funded additional midway research on messaging, print costs for the *In Her Shoes* booklet of stories, and further national newspaper advertising for the final week.

On the day of the vote a group in HQ provided updates on how busy polling stations were throughout the day. It was clear from early on that turnout was good but uncertainty remained as to whether this was good or bad for the campaign. Areas where there was low turnout were flagged up and effort was put in on social media to try to boost voter turnout.

Orla remembers voting being a lovely experience. She brought her young son, Adam, with her to their local polling station. There were a lot of young women working there on the day:

"I had my T-shirt on, but a jacket on over it. I had voted, but as I was walking out one young woman on the polling desk recognised me and she just crossed her fingers. I could see it really meant so much to her. It was just one of those moments. It was brilliant."

Polls were due to close at 10 p.m. that night and there were to be two exit polls published shortly afterwards conducted by independent research companies for the *Irish Times* and RTE. That evening, two statements were being discussed at a meeting in HQ. They were drawn up by Silke Paasche and Mark Garrett – one was for a win and the other for a loss. The latter didn't dwell too much on detail, simply stating that despite the No vote abortion would still be a reality in Ireland. Then there were the national newspaper ads that had been prepared by Gráinne first thing that morning – one a thank you for a Yes vote, but also one for a No. As Gráinne recalled:

"The No had been very difficult to draft. What would we say to the country if we lost? What would we say to the women still travelling? They were going into all the papers on the Sunday and Monday so both versions had to be submitted to the papers in advance. It was all slightly surreal."

There was also discussion about how best to care for volunteers throughout the next day if the vote was tight. But as it got later in the day people gathered in a room in HQ where large TV screens had been put up and drinks and food had been laid on. As time went on numbers grew and the building got more jammed. There were some informal speeches with thank yous all round and flowers for the co-directors. As the time for the exit poll approached nerves were stretched. Everyone kept refreshing their phone to see if the results had landed. They landed first on the phone of Nikki Gallagher, a member of the strategic advisory group. She passed her phone to the campaign manager, Deirdre Duffy, who had a microphone and read out the results of the *Irish Times* exit poll. The IPSOS/MRBI poll suggested that the margin of victory for the Yes side would be 68 per cent to 32 per cent. Everyone was euphoric.

What Ailbhe remembered was everyone starting to cry. She began telling those around her that it was a win and they didn't have to cry. "They were telling me, 'Ailbhe we're crying from emotion.'" She laughs as she remembers her own reaction:

> "At that point I was still in automaton mode, with all my emotions under tight control. But I was thinking to myself, quite stunned, 'hmm, we may have a very big win here.' Then the second exit poll came out with much the same result and, you know, it was simply incredible."

Sarah Monaghan remembers it as "the best feeling in the world that we'd actually done it, not just done it, but that the Yes was so high":

> "I don't know what it was like, it was like hysteria. Everyone was laughing, crying, screaming. It was incredible. There's a picture of me standing in that room ... everybody is hugging each other and I'm standing in the middle bawling crying; I'm almost hugging myself. It's the funniest photo. I'm looking like the loneliest campaigner ever. It had just been such a long slog and everyone had taken so much, taking such personal hits and given so much of their personal lives, their relationships and their whatever. So it was a massive release. It was just like 'oh my God it was all worth it.'"

But Gráinne was more cautious in her response. She was hugely relieved to hear the first poll "and that it looked like it was clearly over the line", but then went back to work on preparations for the next day. When the RTE poll was released a short while later reality did begin to dawn. That poll by Behaviour & Attitudes found a massive vote in favour of removing the Eighth Amendment from the Constitution, across all regions of the country, predicting 69.4 per cent in favour of changing the Constitution, with 30.6 per cent against. Gráinne recalled:

"It was kind of the slow realisation that we've actually won, that tomorrow we're going to be winning a referendum. People went absolutely mental. There were tears, just completely ecstatic. Absolutely incredible. But I wasn't able to get to that point; I just couldn't. It wasn't until the next day when I saw the votes being counted that it hit me."

Minister for Health Simon Harris turned up at HQ, as did Minister for Children Katherine Zappone, and Sinn Féin leader Mary Lou McDonald. Later a video would emerge taken by someone who had been passing by HQ. You could hear the shouting and singing from inside. The Voices for Choice choir were in full swing with HQ all lit up and the big Yes at the front of it.

Orla remembered Katherine Zappone's arrival. "She gave me a hug and she was saying 'I think this is the best thing that NWCI has ever done'", said Orla.

"It was just an amazing feeling. The speeches that had just been written didn't capture it at all and I remember Mark Garrett saying they would have to be scrapped. It was the scale of it, what it meant for Ireland, what it meant for women. It was about abortion and also about much more for women in Ireland."

A party was getting underway but Orla got a call then asking her to go on *Morning Ireland*, RTE's current affairs breakfast programme, so she didn't stay late. Before she left Noel Whelan advised her that once she got to that radio studio in the morning to be prepared for the quick switch from the campaigners and the campaign that had just been run so successfully to the political implications of the Yes vote and to the politicians:

"He told me to say whatever I wanted in the morning. But that the narrative would shift .... He said by one o'clock that's what people are going to be talking about. I don't think I realised how quickly that would happen. It was a lovely feeling to go into *Morning Ireland*. People were congratulating me and the

> campaign and it was a lovely moment. But then straightaway it was into the exit poll and commentary that, 'As people had said to the [exit] pollsters that they were always pro-choice anyway, had the campaign made any difference? Was there a need for a campaign at all?' I found it hard to believe."

But afterwards, for Orla, walking into the main Dublin count centre in the RDS with her two co-directors "will be one of those best feelings forever":

> "It was a little bit intimidating in terms of all the international media in our faces, but it was incredible. I got a few minutes literally just to walk round the hall. And it was just amazing seeing all the Yes bundles. That was one of my favourite moments of the day."

Gráinne, who returned to the RDS with her co-directors later that morning, had already slipped quietly in when it opened that morning, and there she finally allowed herself to fully believe and absorb the scale of the success:

> "It was only when I actually saw them counting out the ballot papers, that it really hit me: we had done it, we had won, every single ballot was somebody who had listened and thought about it and taken the time to vote Yes, and it was a landslide. That was definitely the most emotional moment for me. As I walked around the hall I met local activists tallying who I hadn't seen since before the campaign began. We just hugged. There was no need to talk; we all knew what it meant."

There was lots of media to be done that day. Ailbhe was over in RTE doing the TV election coverage, and later bumped into John McGuirk of the Save the 8th campaign as she left Newstalk after an interview:

> "We met outside. He very graciously turned to me and said, 'Well done, you fought a very good campaign.' I thanked him

and said I had been on the losing side so often I knew how hard
it was to lose. I was impressed by that because I had done a
couple of radio debates with him, and he certainly was our bête
noire."

The next public event for the three co-directors was Dublin Castle,
where the result would be announced. This had been the location
of the incredibly heart-warming scenes following the result of the
marriage equality referendum in 2015. There was a public event on
that occasion where people crowded into the courtyard.

But in the days running up to the vote nobody was sure how this
particular result was going to be handled. Who should be making
the decision about an event in the courtyard of Dublin Castle?
Should Together for Yes request it, or was it under the Government's control? Anyway there had been mixed signals coming from
Fine Gael about what might happen. The ambivalence that had
marked the party's campaign and the fear of striking the wrong note
– despite what was shaping up to be a massive win – continued to
prevail. Ailbhe believes the Government was afraid there could be
trouble:

"I'm speculating but even on the morning of the count we didn't
know if Dublin Castle was going to be opened up to the general
public and I was not at all pleased about that."

In the early afternoon, when she was finishing up various interviews,
she finally got word to come to Dublin Castle and was driven there
by Dermo. It was only as they approached that she realised that the
Upper Castle Yard, the elegant, historic cobblestoned square, was
packed:

"I will never, ever forget that in my life. The people standing
and clapping; it brings tears to my eyes now. It didn't at the
time; I was totally overcome to hear people shouting my name.
I couldn't believe it. It was the most moving thing possible – like
the Red Sea opening up. I couldn't walk very well that day with

> my back, so Dermo was carrying my bag on his arm and asking people to give me space. They just wanted to hug me. It was absolutely wonderful. I had this absolutely massive sense of relief."

Gráinne remembers the absolute joy of those gathered:

> "It was just so lovely to be there, to see the joy radiating out of this crowd of young women. I could see ARC campaigners and friends throughout the crowd. Everyone could feel that it was about so much more than abortion. Women felt recognised, valued and for so many who were treated terribly there was a form of justice, of validation, in the result."

A long stage, spanning the top of the castle yard, had been set up, but somewhat incredibly there was no amplification. For Orla the feeling of joy from the mainly female crowd gathered that afternoon, many of them the young women who had played such an active role in the campaign, seemed like such a statement about women's rights in Ireland. In the crowd at least one woman had brought along and was handing out mint chocolates from her box of After Eights, the new treat of choice for Repealers — a fact which quickly made its way onto social media. Spotting a marketing opportunity, the makers of the mint thins quickly tweeted, "We best get some more supplies to Ireland." As Orla said:

> "It was so much about our time has come. It was about so many different things I think, particularly for young women as well. It was about women not being treated as second-class citizens anymore. It was a real feeling of 'now we're taking our rightful place.'"

The three co-directors were on stage and received massive cheers, as did Health Minister Simon Harris, who had gained a huge following among young women impressed with his work on the campaign. The recently married minister emerged somewhat incongruously as a sex symbol in an abortion campaign. 'I fancy Simon Harris' signs could be seen from the stage.

Quite ridiculously, no sound system had been put in place. They ended up, as Ailbhe remarked, doing "a kind of semaphore on the stage; you know, like a cabin crew member. It was completely mad." After all those decades of fighting for abortion in Ireland they were just hours away from the official announcement of a landslide vote and the women who had run this hugely successful campaign could not be heard. However there was no shortage of applause and cheering from the ecstatic crowd that had gathered.

The official result happened downstairs in a conference room in Dublin Castle – announced in a low-key manner, especially in comparison to the jubilant scenes going on up above. The Yes side won the referendum by 66.4 per cent to 33.6 per cent per cent. The total valid poll was 2,153,613, with 1,429,981 in favour of repealing and 723,632 against. It was a stunning victory.

Gráinne wasn't with her team downstairs; instead she watched the crowd in Dublin Castle from the stage as they erupted with the victory announcement – luckily somebody had worked out some form of amplification for that. She had been asked by RTE, as a co-director of the campaign, to be there to respond to the result. However after having her on standby she was surprised to see them move immediately after the announcement to Labour Senator Aodhán Ó Ríordáin. They didn't come back to her.

Gráinne didn't mind missing the formal announcement, treasuring the sight of the crowd reacting. However, she did take a member of the RTE production team aside and point out that in the aftermath of the landslide referendum victory result, delivered by the most astonishing movement for women's reproductive rights ever seen in Ireland, he had chosen to go to a male senator, who wasn't centrally involved, for comment, rather than the female co-leader of the referendum campaign.

"His face fell; it hadn't dawned on him at all", she said. He offered to 'make it up' by interviewing her with Cora Sherlock (Love Both spokeswoman) in the Rose Garden in Dublin Castle. She refused. Having just won the referendum, it was finally no longer about the other side and she certainly wasn't going head-to-head with any of them. In hindsight, Gráinne felt the interaction was typical of the approach much of the mainstream media took to the campaign.

On the way back to the hotel in Ballsbridge where the campaign had based itself, the co-directors readied themselves for the next phase of the day. Ailbhe was happy with her speech, drafted by Sinéad Kennedy and herself, but Orla and Gráinne were frantically scribbling speeches to give to all of the volunteers and supporters who had gathered there. All three remember feeling so tired they almost wanted to collapse. But then they saw the crowd and were buoyed up once more.

The three co-directors gave their speeches and there was jubilation in the room. Then word came quite late that the Taoiseach and Minister for Health were arriving; a number of supporters had left at that point but the big room was closed off and a smaller room was used to make it still look like a good crowd. Both men congratulated Together for Yes very warmly and were clearly delighted at the scale of the result.

Orla was very disappointed to miss that part as she had to leave to collect her son. Ailbhe remembers the Taoiseach being very gracious, saying something along the lines of some people had been working on the issue long before it was acceptable to do so:

> "There was a real acknowledgement that there was a time when you were a pariah if you fought for women's right to choose, and suddenly we were no longer pariahs. Quite a turnaround."

Angela Coraccio from ARC had arranged an after-party in a city centre venue. The versatile Dermo had moved from chauffeuring to DJing. As Gráinne remembered:

> "I could barely stand at that point from exhaustion but I walked in and saw the faces and it was like coming home, they were my people. So many wonderful, beautiful people who had given so much and whom I had worked with for years to get to that day, to get to Repeal. I found a stool in the corner and watched

people going wild on the dancefloor underneath photos of the last six years scrolling by on a slideshow, I was so tired, so happy, and just so relieved, so relieved we had won and so relieved it was over."

For Orla that party was a great reflection of what had gone on in the months previously as she watched everyone mixing together in celebration:

"To me it really sort of showed how things had totally come around, the relationships that were built and the friendships. ARC and NWCI were probably the two organisations most sceptical of each other. I think some people in ARC would have been critical of the Women's Council for being seen as too mainstream, and us being concerned would they ever keep to message. It was just a great night because you could just really see that things had shifted. This woman came over to me and said, 'I've never wanted to support the Women's Council but you're our Women's Council now', and gave me a big hug. It was just lovely."

Sarah Monaghan left with her boyfriend, Peter, and as they were walking home towards Rathmines they came across the Savita Halappanavar mural, which had been erected on Lennox Street. It was close to where they had had their party. Candles were lighting. Coincidentally there were around ten other ARC women there, whom Sarah had worked with for years, also on the way home, as well as other people who had gathered:

"That floored me to be honest. It just took the knees from under me and we were all bawling crying standing there. We didn't speak, but it was incredibly powerful. I remember as we walked away saying to Peter something along the lines of 'I'm just so sorry it was too late for her.' It was a really beautiful and immensely powerful unorchestrated moment. We did it. We got there. But it is unfortunately always just a little bit tinged with sadness that it was too late for her and so many others."

The final official engagement for the Together for Yes campaign was a press conference on the Sunday morning. Journalist Gerry Foley from TV3 broke the ice by asking who had gotten home the latest from the previous evening's celebrations. Orla recalled:

"Everything was very serious at first but there was a lovely moment when Gerry asked that question and we all laughed. There's a really nice photo of it. You could see the relaxation on our faces. We were bringing things to a close that morning. We thanked the media as well, the journalists who were present who had covered it and the way we felt, leaving aside a few – they had covered it really well."

NWCI, at its next AGM, would present a framed copy of that photograph to Gráinne and Ailbhe.

Looking back, Orla believes that while you cannot put in enough preparation for a campaign you also have to be prepared for the unexpected:

"It would be fair to say that for myself, Ailbhe and Gráinne we like to have things under control. But you can't control everything and you have to live with that and go with it and not get too stressed about it. I think that will be one of my learnings in terms of how I approach things since the referendum. You just have to be agile enough to reassess and move when you need to. The referendum campaign makes me optimistic about change for women in Ireland. But only if we go about it in a particular way. And it takes time.

The one thing that was clear is the importance of that personal story in convincing people of the need for change. What I learned from the campaign is that if you can talk about really difficult issues in a way that speaks to the values of people and the compassionate part of people – and not keep repeating your demand and expect them to think you're right – then you have a really good chance of succeeding. When I look now at campaigns I think in the main that's why a lot of campaigns fail. It's trying to force people into that thing – 'if I'm right, you're wrong. You've got to agree with me.' That just doesn't work. I also think you can never underestimate the resistance to change so, as all feminists know, we have to be in it for the long haul."

What about that RTE exit poll, which asked three key questions relating to the campaign in terms of when people had made up their minds on abortion, or if they had changed their minds during the course of the campaign? Across the three questions a large majority, up to 82 per cent, indicated that, in essence, they had decided long before the campaign; in fact before the Citizens' Assembly or the Oireachtas Committee on the Eighth Amendment or indeed the death of Savita Halappanavar. The poll also indicated that 43 per cent of Yes voters quoted 'personal stories in the media' as their reason for voting Yes.

Unsurprisingly, and with considerable logic, the three co-directors in many ways understood the answers, but also believe that it is a more complex situation than that presented by the poll. This is especially given the findings of their own detailed research, including those focus groups and the 'concerned centre', which they knew existed among the voters. They had also seen a narrowing of the opinion polls against abortion. The referendum had the third highest turnout ever recorded, at 64.13 per cent. This had been civil society putting a line down for the Government and persisting with it until it had agreed to put the abortion question to the Irish people. The country had changed and two-thirds of people voted to indicate that notable change. The strength of that statement indicated that 'old Ireland' was dead and gone.

For Orla it was obvious that people had been going back and forth in their thinking and that this was reflected in what they heard back from the canvassing during the campaign:

"The canvassers were telling us about the conversations with people. It was 'yeah I do agree with it, but ...'. And that is also what we saw from our focus group research. So then I think in the last week when they made up their minds, it was 'well I sort of always thought that way.' What we saw from the focus groups and the door-to-door canvassing, that gives me lots of optimism for future change, is that people were prepared to support women when the harm and devastation to women's and couples' lives was made apparent to them. But they did struggle with it, saying they were uncomfortable with abortion. But I do not believe for one second if there hadn't been the Together for Yes campaign we would have seen that result .... I think the chances are we would've won it, but we might also have lost out by a small margin. We certainly wouldn't have achieved the scale of the turnout and the vote."

Ailbhe believes the Irish people were waiting to be asked the right question:

"After the death of Savita Halappanavar, they may have made their minds up, but they didn't know that until they were asked what they actually thought, and what they really wanted. Somebody had to come along and re-frame the question, ask them if they wanted to repeal the Eighth Amendment, and put an end to tragedy, to decades of unnecessary suffering, humiliation, and hypocrisy. They had to have an opportunity to look at the reality of women's lives, including abortion, and to think and talk honestly about that. That's what a referendum campaign does – it's a huge national conversation. When you look at the momentum of a big campaign you see that as it grows stronger and more persuasive, people think that they've always thought that way. We had avoided and denied and pushed the question of abortion under the carpet for so long that people were afraid to look at it at all, and someone – that was us in the Repeal movement – had to bring it up into the light. Quite honestly, I don't think any government was going to ask that question unless they were forced, and we forced them to do so."

A few days after the win, Gráinne was at home with her friend Aoife Cooke, home from Australia. Friends since UCD student days, Aoife had stayed with Gráinne the previous few weeks, but they hardly saw each other, both were so busy. Aoife's dad, Jim Cooke, a retired school teacher, came to collect her. Gráinne remembers how delighted he was with the referendum result. She was a little surprised, not realising it would be so important to him. He sat down and told his own story of the Eighth Amendment, of Aoife's late mother and when she was diagnosed with a brain tumour. The doctor required her to do a pregnancy test. It was negative.

"It wasn't long after the 1983 referendum but he didn't make the connection with the Amendment at the time, but he did realise that if the pregnancy test had been positive the treatment plan they were discussing wouldn't have been going ahead. He said something at the time like, 'What are you talking about, that we wouldn't be discussing this treatment plan? Well we would be going to England.' But he didn't have the time to even think about it then because he was dealing with his young wife dying of cancer and parenting four young kids. Later, he was really angry about it and he was just absolutely thrilled with the Yes vote. After he left I found an envelope on my kitchen table with 'Gráinne' on the front. Inside was a cheque for €100.

I called Aoife and she explained that her dad wanted me to get myself something for all the time I had taken off work and all the work I had put into the referendum. I was incredibly touched. But you know there were stories like his just packaged up in every house in Ireland and just kind of set aside, and then during those weeks they were taken back out. I felt like people were offering them up, like a weight they had been carrying around for decades. It was really extraordinary to watch, that kind of catharsis within a society. It was something I stopped and noticed, felt, at certain points. It was so deeply moving. Those were the real moments of the campaign, not the debates or the polls or anything like that."

Coming up to the first anniversary of the referendum in May 2019, the three co-directors – Gráinne Griffin, Orla O'Connor and Ailbhe Smyth – were included on the 2019 *Time* 100 Most Influential People list. Irish actress Ruth Negga wrote the citation. She explained that on 25 May 2018, Irish society gave its overwhelming blessing to the fundamental rights of women and girls to bodily autonomy, after generations of secondary status, largely dictated by the power and oppression of the Catholic Church:

"Together for Yes, the campaign to repeal the eighth amend-ment to the Irish constitution, put the Mná na hÉireann (women of Ireland) front, center [sic] and in control of their own bodies and rights like never before. It was breathtaking to witness the determination, intelligence and sheer hard work of its leaders, Gráinne Griffin, Ailbhe Smyth and Orla O'Connor, who mobi-lized people of all different backgrounds in the lead-up to the vote. They put the experiences of women and the needs of their country first.

Their incredible tenacity and integrity and courageousness will be an inspiration for generations to come."